325.731
CVL

Cuban Immigration

Roger E. Hernández

THE CHANGING
Face of North America:
IMMIGRATION SINCE 1965

HPHS Library

CUBAN IMMIGRATION

OCT 08

Langston Hughes Community
Library and Cultural Center
100-01 Northern Boulevard
Corona, NY 11368

Roger E. Hernández

MASON CREST PUBLISHERS
PHILADELPHIA

Produced by OTTN Publishing, Stockton, New Jersey

Mason Crest Publishers
370 Reed Road
Broomall, PA 19008
www.masoncrest.com

Copyright © 2004 by Mason Crest Publishers. All rights reserved.
Printed and bound in the Hashemite Kingdom of Jordan.

First printing

1 3 5 7 9 8 6 4 2

Library of Congress Cataloging-in-Publication Data

Hernández, Roger E.
  Cuban immigration / Roger E. Hernández.
      p. cm. — (The changing face of North America)
Summary: An overview of immigration from Cuba to the United States and Canada since the 1960s, when immigra-
tion laws were changed to permit greater numbers of people to enter these countries.
Includes bibliographical references (p.) and index.
  ISBN 1-59084-681-8
1. Cuban Americans—History—20th century—Juvenile literature. 2. Cubans—Canada—History—20th century—
Juvenile literature. 3. Immigrants—United States—History—20th century—Juvenile literature.
4. Immigrants—Canada—History—20th century—Juvenile literature. 5. Cuba—Emigration and immigration—
History—20th century—Juvenile literature. 6. United States—Emigration and immigration—History—20th
century—Juvenile literature. 7. Canada—Emigration and immigration—History—20th century—Juvenile literature.
[1. Cuban Americans—History—20th century. 2. Cubans—Canada—History—20th century. 3. Immigrants—
United States—History—20th century. 4. Immigrants—Canada—History—20th century. 5. Cuba—Emigration and
immigration—History—20th century. 6. United States—Emigration and immigration—History—20th century.
7. Canada—Emigration and immigration—History—20th century.] I. Title. II. Series.
  E184.C97H47 2004
  304.8'7307291—dc22
                                                                                        2003016370

THE CHANGING
Face of North America:
IMMIGRATION SINCE 1965

CONTENTS

INTRODUCTION

THE CHANGING FACE OF AMERICA

By Senator Edward M. Kennedy

America is proud of its heritage and history as a nation of immigrants, and my own family is an example. All eight of my great-grandparents were immigrants who left Ireland a century and a half ago, when that land was devastated by the massive famine caused by the potato blight. When I was a young boy, my grandfather used to take me down to the docks in Boston and regale me with stories about the Great Famine and the waves of Irish immigrants who came to America seeking a better life. He talked of how the Irish left their marks in Boston and across the nation, enduring many hardships and harsh discrimination, but also building the railroads, digging the canals, settling the West, and filling the factories of a growing America. According to one well-known saying of the time, "under every railroad tie, an Irishman is buried."

America was the promised land for them, as it has been for so many other immigrants who have found shelter, hope, opportunity, and freedom. Immigrants have always been an indispensable part of our nation. They have contributed immensely to our communities, created new jobs and whole new industries, served in our armed forces, and helped make America the continuing land of promise that it is today.

The inspiring poem by Emma Lazarus, inscribed on the pedestal of the Statue of Liberty in New York Harbor, is America's welcome to all immigrants:

Give me your tired, your poor,
Your huddled masses yearning to breathe free,
The wretched refuse of your teeming shore,
Send these, the homeless, tempest-tossed, to me:
I lift my lamp beside the golden door.

The period since September 11, 2001, has been particularly challenging for immigrants. Since the horrifying terrorist attacks, there has been a resurgence of anti-immigrant attitudes and behavior. We all agree that our borders must be safe and secure. Yet, at the same time, we must safeguard the entry of the millions of persons who come to the United States legally each year as immigrants, visitors, scholars, students, and workers. The "golden door" must stay open. We must recognize that immigration is not the problem—terrorism is. We must identify and isolate the terrorists, and not isolate America.

One of my most important responsibilities in the Senate is the preservation of basic rights and basic fairness in the application of our immigration laws, so that new generations of immigrants in our own time and for all time will have the same opportunity that my great-grandparents had when they arrived in America.

Immigration is beneficial for the United States and for countries throughout the world. It is no coincidence that two hundred years ago, our nations' founders chose *E Pluribus Unum*—"out of many, one"—as America's motto. These words, chosen by Benjamin Franklin, John Adams, and Thomas Jefferson, refer to the ideal that separate colonies can be transformed into one united nation. Today, this ideal has come to apply to individuals as well. Our diversity is our strength. We are a nation of immigrants, and we always will be.

FOREWORD

THE CHANGING FACE OF THE UNITED STATES

Marian L. Smith, historian
U.S. Immigration and Naturalization Service

Americans commonly assume that immigration today is very different than immigration of the past. The immigrants themselves appear to be unlike immigrants of earlier eras. Their language, their dress, their food, and their ways seem strange. At times people fear too many of these new immigrants will destroy the America they know. But has anything really changed? Do new immigrants have any different effect on America than old immigrants a century ago? Is the American fear of too much immigration a new development? Do immigrants really change America more than America changes the immigrants? The very subject of immigration raises many questions.

In the United States, immigration is more than a chapter in a history book. It is a continuous thread that links the present moment to the first settlers on North American shores. From the first colonists' arrival until today, immigrants have been met by Americans who both welcomed and feared them. Immigrant contributions were always welcome—on the farm, in the fields, and in the factories. Welcoming the poor, the persecuted, and the "huddled masses" became an American principle. Beginning with the original Pilgrims' flight from religious persecution in the 1600s, through the Irish migration to escape starvation in the 1800s, to the relocation of Central Americans seeking refuge from civil wars in the 1980s and 1990s, the United States has considered itself a haven for the destitute and the oppressed.

But there was also concern that immigrants would not adopt American ways, habits, or language. Too many immigrants might overwhelm America. If so, the dream of the Founding Fathers for United States government and society would be destroyed. For this reason, throughout American history some have argued that limiting or ending immigration is our patriotic duty. Benjamin Franklin feared there were so many German immigrants in Pennsylvania the Colonial Legislature would begin speaking German. "Progressive" leaders of the early 1900s feared that immigrants who could not read and understand the English language were not only exploited by "big business," but also served as the foundation for "machine politics" that undermined the U.S. Constitution. This theme continues today, usually voiced by those who bear no malice toward immigrants but who want to preserve American ideals.

Have immigrants changed? In colonial days, when most colonists were of English descent, they considered Germans, Swiss, and French immigrants as different. They were not "one of us" because they spoke a different language. Generations later, Americans of German or French descent viewed Polish, Italian, and Russian immigrants as strange. They were not "like us" because they had a different religion, or because they did not come from a tradition of constitutional government. Recently, Americans of Polish or Italian descent have seen Nicaraguan, Pakistani, or Vietnamese immigrants as too different to be included. It has long been said of American immigration that the latest ones to arrive usually want to close the door behind them.

It is important to remember that fear of individual immigrant groups seldom lasted, and always lessened. Benjamin Franklin's anxiety over German immigrants disappeared after those immigrants' sons and daughters helped the nation gain independence in the Revolutionary War. The Irish of the mid-1800s were among the most hated immigrants, but today we all wear green on St. Patrick's Day. While a century ago it was feared that Italian and other Catholic immigrants would vote as directed by the Pope, today that controversy is only a vague memory. Unfortunately, some ethnic groups continue their efforts to earn acceptance. The African

Americans' struggle continues, and some Asian Americans, whose families have been in America for generations, are the victims of current anti-immigrant sentiment.

Time changes both immigrants and America. Each wave of new immigrants, with their strange language and habits, eventually grows old and passes away. Their American-born children speak English. The immigrants' grandchildren are completely American. The strange foods of their ancestors—spaghetti, baklava, hummus, or tofu—become common in any American restaurant or grocery store. Much of what the immigrants brought to these shores is lost, principally their language. And what is gained becomes as American as St. Patrick's Day, Hanukkah, or Cinco de Mayo, and we forget that it was once something foreign.

Recent immigrants are all around us. They come from every corner of the earth to join in the American Dream. They will continue to help make the American Dream a reality, just as all the immigrants who came before them have done.

FOREWORD

THE CHANGING FACE OF CANADA

Peter A. Hammerschmidt
First Secretary, Permanent Mission of Canada to the United Nations

Throughout Canada's history, immigration has shaped and defined the very character of Canadian society. The migration of peoples from every part of the world into Canada has profoundly changed the way we look, speak, eat, and live. Through close and distant relatives who left their lands in search of a better life, all Canadians have links to immigrant pasts. We are a nation built by and of immigrants.

Two parallel forces have shaped the history of Canadian immigration. The enormous diversity of Canada's immigrant population is the most obvious. In the beginning came the enterprising settlers of the "New World," the French and English colonists. Soon after came the Scottish, Irish, and Northern and Central European farmers of the 1700s and 1800s. As the country expanded westward during the mid-1800s, migrant workers began arriving from China, Japan, and other Asian countries. And the turbulent twentieth century brought an even greater variety of immigrants to Canada, from the Caribbean, Africa, India, and Southeast Asia.

So while English- and French-Canadians are the largest ethnic groups in the country today, neither group alone represents a majority of the population. A large and vibrant multicultural mix makes up the rest, particularly in Canada's major cities. Toronto, Vancouver, and Montreal alone are home to people from over 200 ethnic groups!

Less obvious but equally important in the evolution of Canadian immigration has been hope. The promise of a better life lured Europeans and Americans seeking cheap (sometimes even free) farmland. Thousands of Scots and Irish arrived to escape grinding poverty and starvation. Others came for freedom, to escape religious and political persecution. Canada has long been a haven to the world's dispossessed and disenfranchised—Dutch and German farmers cast out for their religious beliefs, black slaves fleeing the United States, and political refugees of despotic regimes in Europe, Africa, Asia, and South America.

The two forces of diversity and hope, so central to Canada's past, also shaped the modern era of Canadian immigration. Following the Second World War, Canada drew heavily on these influences to forge trailblazing immigration initiatives.

The catalyst for change was the adoption of the Canadian Bill of Rights in 1960. Recognizing its growing diversity and Canadians' changing attitudes towards racism, the government passed a federal statute barring discrimination on the grounds of race, national origin, color, religion, or sex. Effectively rejecting the discriminatory elements in Canadian immigration policy, the Bill of Rights forced the introduction of a new policy in 1962. The focus of immigration abruptly switched from national origin to the individual's potential contribution to Canadian society. The door to Canada was now open to every corner of the world.

Welcoming those seeking new hopes in a new land has also been a feature of Canadian immigration in the modern era. The focus on economic immigration has increased along with Canada's steadily growing economy, but political immigration has also been encouraged. Since 1945, Canada has admitted tens of thousands of displaced persons, including Jewish Holocaust survivors, victims of Soviet crackdowns in Hungary and Czechoslovakia, and refugees from political upheaval in Uganda, Chile, and Vietnam.

Prior to 1978, however, these political refugees were admitted as an exception to normal immigration procedures. That year, Canada revamped its refugee policy with a new Immigration Act that explicitly affirmed Canada's commitment to the resettlement of refugees from oppression. Today, the admission of refugees remains a central part of Canadian immigration law and regulations.

Amendments to economic and political immigration policy continued during the 1980s and 1990s, refining further the bold steps taken during the modern era. Together, these initiatives have turned Canada into one of the world's few truly multicultural states.

Unlike the process of assimilation into a "melting pot" of cultures, immigrants to Canada are more likely to retain their cultural identity, beliefs, and practices. This is the source of some of Canada's greatest strengths as a society. And as a truly multicultural nation, diversity is not seen as a threat to Canadian identity. Quite the contrary—diversity *is* Canadian identity.

1 SUCCESS AND SADNESS

There aren't many groups that have moved toward attaining the "American dream" as rapidly as the Cuban exiles. But there aren't many groups, either, that have a stronger affinity for the homeland they had to leave behind.

The first major exodus from Cuba, an island nation less than 100 miles (161 kilometers) from the Florida Keys, brought exiles to North America during the early 1960s. Nearly everyone came to get away from the regime of Fidel Castro, who took power in 1959. Since then, other Cubans have been seeking freedoms denied them in their native country.

Only a small number of Cubans has settled in Canada. As of Canada's 2001 census, there were 5,320 Cuban-born people living in the country, about half of whom arrived after 1996. Because of their small numbers, Cubans living in Canada have not made a large impact on Canadian life, although defections of small Cuban groups in 1998 and in 2002 have raised some national awareness of the exiles' situation. A much larger number of Cubans has resettled in the United States, where, according to the 2000 U.S. Census, 1.2 million people of Cuban ancestry live. It is in the United States that Cuban exiles and their American-born children have had the strongest impact.

◀ A U.S. Navy ship transports Cuban refugees to the naval base at Guantánamo Bay, Cuba, after they are picked up at sea, August 1994. Since the early 1960s, large waves of Cuban refugees have left for Canada and the United States seeking freedom. They have traveled by plane, ship, and even makeshift boats and rafts.

The Waves of Cuban Immigration

Most members of the first exile group came by airplane. Though they were considered the elite of their nation, they arrived penniless because the Castro government only permitted them to bring a couple of changes of clothes. Those who could not travel by airplane braved the treacherous waters of the Florida Straits in homemade rafts, taking with them just barely enough food and water to survive the voyage. Most of them arrived in Miami, the closest major city to Cuba.

At first, the exiles were unable to practice their professions and had to take whatever low-paying jobs they could find so that their families would have the necessary provisions. Stories abound in the Cuban community about surgeons who cleaned toilets, or professors who worked in small retail shops, earning little more than American teenagers did at a part-time job.

By the end of the 1960s, however, many Cuban immigrants had started their own businesses, and the group's professionals reestablished themselves. As years went on, they were joined by other immigrating Cubans, who had less formal education but were just as eager to succeed.

The first wave of Cuban immigrants did not stray far from its roots, but the majority of the sons and daughters—who had come from Cuba as children or were born in the United States during their parents' years of struggle—grew up bilingual and bicultural. By the 1970s and 1980s, many individuals in this second generation had graduated from college and begun their own careers. Those with children were parents to a generation that only knew life in America, two whole generations removed from the turbulent period of Castro's rise to power.

Today, severe economic hardship is a mostly thing of the past for most Cuban immigrant families. In terms of socioeconomic indicators such as average income, education, and home ownership, the estimated 1.2 million people of Cuban ancestry who live in the United States are not very different from the non-Hispanic white population. In other words, even though the post-1959 Cuban immigrant group has been in the

United States for just a generation or two, they have quickly reached a level of success comparable to that of American families who have been in the country much longer.

What's more, Cuban Americans have become a powerful political, cultural, and economic force. At the national level, many political observers say, the Cuban American vote gave George W. Bush the edge that put him over the top in the presidential election of 2000. At the local level, Cubans have left their mark on Miami, a city where speaking Spanish is as common as speaking English, even in the wealthiest neighborhoods and the most prominent executive boardrooms. In Miami, Cuban Americans run businesses large and small, Cuban American artists comprise an important part of the cultural

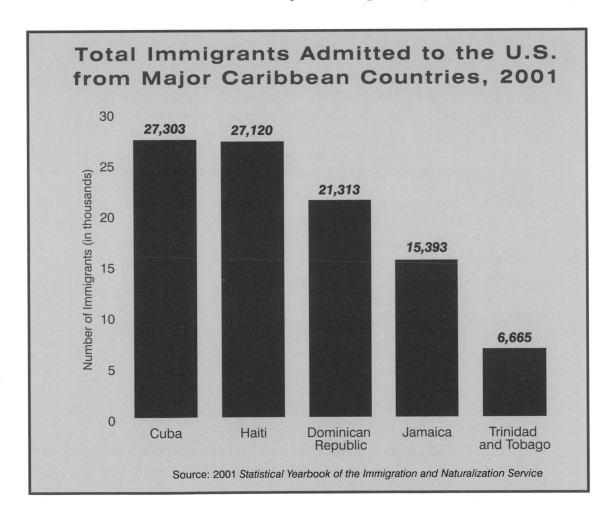

Total Immigrants Admitted to the U.S. from Major Caribbean Countries, 2001

Number of Immigrants (in thousands)

Cuba	Haiti	Dominican Republic	Jamaica	Trinidad and Tobago
27,303	27,120	21,313	15,393	6,665

Source: 2001 *Statistical Yearbook of the Immigration and Naturalization Service* scene, and Cuban American politicians are consistently elected to municipal office, the Florida legislature, and U.S. Congress.

Remembering the Homeland

Yet for all these forms of success, many Cuban Americans by and large feel a great sadness. Cuban immigrants are grateful that they could resettle during a time of need, and that they found opportunities that allowed them and their children to succeed, yet many still long for the Cuba they had to leave behind.

The sons and daughters of the original exiles assimilated more easily, yet they grew up listening to their parents' stories

Ethnicity and Race

The major ethnic categories of North Americans are white, black, Asian, Native American, and Hispanic. Since ethnicity and race are often used interchangeably to describe people, it may be confusing to hear that a Hispanic person can also be white, black, Native American, or Asian.

To dispel the confusion, it is important to first recognize that the Hispanic population encompasses a wide range of people. Cubans, for example, are just one group of many referred to as "Hispanic" (many people from Latin American countries or of Latin American descent prefer the term *Latino*). The term *Hispanic* also refers to Argentineans, Mexicans, Puerto Ricans, Nicaraguans, Spaniards, or any people born in—or trace their heritage to—any of the world's 20 Spanish-speaking lands. Hispanics thus include people of every color who share specific historical and cultural attributes, but they do not form a single race.

Like the United States and Canada, most Hispanic countries are made up of people of different races who have close or distant ties to other countries. In Cuba, the largest racial groups are whites and blacks. The majority of white Cubans are the descendants of Spaniards who immigrated to Cuba while it was a Spanish colony or during its first decades as an independent state. But there are also Cubans whose ancestors arrived on the island after leaving Italy, Ireland, England, and even China. Cuba also had a significant Jewish population.

Cuba's other large population is of African ancestry. In the United States and in Cuba, a significant number of black people trace their lineage to enslaved Africans brought to work on the plantations.

Many young Cuban Americans wrestle with their own cultural identity. Unlike their parents and grandparents, Cuban American children may only know life in the United States, yet many still try to preserve their heritage through speaking Spanish and participating in Cuban festivals.

of loss. Many who have received this mixed heritage struggle with what it means to be an American of Cuban descent, and are thus are faced with pressing questions: How different are we, really, from other Americans? Should our main language be English or Spanish? How committed should we be to bringing democracy to Cuba?

Finally, there are the issues facing the youngest generation, the grandchildren of those who left Cuba as adults, those born in America and who only know life in the United States. Of course, as children they ask more basic questions: Should I learn enough Spanish to speak to my grandparents? Do I want hamburger for dinner, or rice with black beans? But upon closer observation, it seems they ask the same question their parents ask themselves: How Cuban am I, and how American? In the end, Cuban Americans have to individually answer that question. But there is no doubt that that their Cuban roots remain with them in some way.

2 Why Cubans Want to Leave

A dominant thread running through Cuban history is the continual search for freedom. For nearly two centuries, Cubans have come to North America to escape political instability and repressive governments in their homeland.

Yet nothing made more Cubans leave their country than Fidel Castro's ascension to power and the institution of his communist regime in 1959. Nearly one-tenth of the population has left since then, mostly to the United States. To understand what enabled Castro to take up power, it is important to become familiar with the nation's basic history.

The recorded history of Cuba began when Columbus landed on the eastern part of the island during his first voyage to the Americas in 1492. After Columbus' landing, the island became a colony of Spain. Spanish settlers founded the major cities, and their Cuban-born descendants populated the island over the next few centuries. When most of the original Amerindian population died from disease or from being overworked, the settlers brought slaves from Africa.

It was this mixture of the African and Spanish that produced the Cuban people, but it took decades for a national identity to develop. From the 1500s until the early 1800s, most Cubans who were not enslaved thought of themselves as Spaniards from Cuba. But the American Revolutionary War and the creation of an independent United States influenced the Cubans' sense of identity as Cubans instead of Spaniards, and about the

◀ Cuban president Fidel Castro delivers a speech in Camagüey, Cuba, announcing victory in the revolution to oust dictator Fulgencio Batista, January 1959. Shortly after the coup Castro instituted his communist regime. One-tenth of the Cuban population has since escaped the repressive system to settle in another country.

possibility of self-rule. These feelings were intensified when Spanish colonial authorities forbade Cuban-born persons to hold high government office in their native land.

By the early 1800s many Cubans had begun to see themselves as Cuban, just as many Americans had seen themselves as Americans during the War for Independence. The Cubans felt they were under the control of a foreign country, Spain, and that they had the right to freely govern themselves as a sovereign state. By 1868, they had decided that self-governance was worth fighting a war for.

The Fight for Independence

The 1850s saw the start of a struggle for freedom that, many Cubans say, has yet to be won. Spanish authorities put down several uprisings and conspiracies. Then in 1868 Cubans began the first of their wars of independence. The Ten Years War, as it came to be called, ended in 1878 with the defeat of Cuban rebel forces and the tremendous devastation to the people and the economy. Nearly a quarter of a million people had been killed, and the large sugar estates on which the economy depended were in ruins.

When the war ended,

José Martí (1853–95), essayist and poet, was an illustrious leader in the Cuban fight for independence during the 1890s. He died fighting in the war against Spain, which began in 1895 and ended in 1898, just months after the United States entered the war on the side of Cuba.

Spain's government promised to permit more self-rule for Cubans, but it soon broke that promise. Cubans felt frustrated because their struggle for freedom had come to nothing. A new war broke out in 1895, under the leadership of the essayist and poet José Martí, a leading figure in Cuba's history.

Martí was killed in battle just weeks after the war began. Fighting dragged on for three years, and in 1898 the USS *Maine*, a battleship that had been sent to Cuba to protect American lives and property from the war's spreading violence, blew up in Havana harbor.

The United States blamed the Spaniards for the disaster and declared war on Spain. Cuban and American troops defeated the Spanish in a few months, ending four centuries of Spanish rule. The United States governed Cuba until May 20, 1902, when the Cuban flag was raised at Havana's ancient Morro Castle in a ceremony that signaled the birth of the independent Republic of Cuba. Many Cubans believed they had reached their goal of complete freedom, though they soon faced another letdown.

The Cuban Republic

Cuba was not yet completely independent because the U.S. government insisted that the Cuban constitution include the Platt Amendment, a clause that permitted Americans to intervene in the instance of a rebellion or revolution that the Cuban government could not control. Many Cubans resented the amendment, considering it an infringement of their sovereign rights.

The U.S. government intervened in Cuba several times—in 1906, 1912, and 1917—in response to the instability of its government. In some cases the U.S. had to respond to complaints of government corruption. However, Cuba showed promise in many ways: a middle class began to grow even in the midst of widespread unemployment. Also, Cuba had developed a free press, citizens were now free to speak out, and political parties competed for their vote. But the Cuban movement for democracy took a major blow in the early 1930s when Gerardo Machado, who had been elected president in 1924, refused to give up power and established a repressive dictatorship.

For the first time since the days of colonization, Cubans were imprisoned simply for disagreeing with the government, and political opponents were murdered by government thugs. Soon a new struggle for freedom began. After a general strike paralyzed the nation, Machado was overthrown in 1933. Fighting among political divisions followed, until an army sergeant named Fulgencio Batista became de facto leader.

Batista made himself general and for the rest of the decade was the power behind puppet leaders. In 1934 the Platt Amendment, which had authorized the U.S. government to intervene in Cuban politics, was abolished, (though the U.S. military did maintain control of a naval base at Guantánamo Bay, located on the island). The abolition of the amendment was very important to Cubans, because they could now say that they were no longer a semi-colony subject to American political and military interference.

Then in 1940, under a new constitution Batista ran for president and won. When his term ended four years later, he stepped down and made way for the elected democratic government of Ramón Grau San Martín, who was followed in 1948 by Carlos Prío Socarrás. Cubans believed that the freedom they had sought since the colonial days had finally arrived.

Under Grau and Prío, the economy grew and democratic practices expanded. Cuba became one of Latin America's most economically advanced nations. But corrupt officials under both presidents stole millions of dollars that should have funded public services such as education and the road network. Using the need to end public corruption as an excuse to regain power, Batista ousted Prío in March 1952 in a golpe de estado (a coup, or sudden seizure of power) and made himself dictator.

Many Cubans had been looking forward to the presidential election that year, with candidates promising to fight corruption, so they were angry to see their hopes of democracy dashed under Batista. In a democracy, citizens at least have the chance to elect new leaders, but Batista's new government permitted no elections or dissent. It censored newspapers and jailed political opponents. As under the Machado administration, government agents had a free hand to imprison or use direct force against those suspected of opposing Batista.

Gerardo Machado (1871–1939) led Cuba in a time of government corruption and political chaos. During his dictatorship, which lasted from 1925 to 1933, Cubans began to migrate from the country to escape persecution as well as to search for better economic opportunities.

The Anti-Batista Resistance

A young lawyer named Fidel Castro was among those opposed to Batista. In 1953 his forces assaulted a military barracks known as Moncada, in the eastern city of Santiago. The attack failed and Castro was imprisoned. But as part of a political amnesty that Batista granted political opponents two years later, Castro was released. He went to Mexico, where he organized another expedition against Batista.

In 1956 Castro and some 80 armed supporters landed on the eastern coast of Cuba. Batista's army hunted down most of the men, but a handful survived, including Castro, his brother Raúl, and Argentinean revolutionary Ernesto "Che" Guevara. The small group fled to the mountains of the Sierra Maestra to hide and regroup.

By this time, Batista became so despised that a number of Cubans decided to help the tiny rebel army. Support grew in the Sierra Maestra as well as in the cities. At this time, Batista's own soldiers were becoming demoralized, and a good number

lost the desire to fight on the side of an unpopular dictator. Castro's men won several skirmishes over the next couple of years, putting Batista's army on the run. Finally, on New Year's Eve, 1958, Batista gave up and fled the country. Castro and his army of revolutionaries entered Havana in triumph.

A week later, more than a million wildly cheering Cubans lined the streets to welcome the rebel army as it paraded through Havana. The vast majority of Cubans treated them like liberating heroes. They thought that, finally, after a century and a half of crushed dreams, Cuba was finally going to be free. They did not know that the new government would become a dictatorship that would impel a million Cubans to leave their homeland.

Cuba Under Castro

Ever since the days of fighting in the mountains against Batista's army, Fidel Castro had promised he would establish a

Argentinean revolutionary Ernesto "Che" Guevara (right) fought alongside Fidel Castro (left) in the early stages of the Cuban Revolution. Following his six years of service in the Cuban government, Guevara led a guerilla movement in Bolivia, where he was killed and became a fallen hero for Latin American communists.

stable democratic government free of corruption—a government that Cubans had always wanted but never had. Castro even came to Washington, D.C., in the spring of 1959 for a televised press conference to reassure his international audience of his democratic plan. "I know you are worried . . . first of all if we are communist," he stated in the address. "And of course . . . I have said very clearly that we are not communist." His words were a promise to many that the democratic, stable, and honest government that Cuba had needed for so long had finally arrived.

However, by the end of the year Castro had ousted most of the moderates from his government and replaced them with communists. In the following months, foreign as well as Cuban-owned businesses were expropriated. Independent newspapers were shut down and replaced by government-owned newspapers that did not criticize Castro. People who protested were put in prison, and many were executed by firing squads.

In the days following Castro's takeover, Batista supporters fled to the United States. Most Cubans were glad Castro's rivals were gone. But as months passed and the Castro regime started to become more dictatorial, many well-to-do Cubans who had placed their hopes on the new government turned against it in disappointment and also fled north.

At that time Cuba's world role was also changing. In May 1960, partly because of ideology and partly due to his resentment of the U.S. government, Castro established close relations with the communist Soviet Union, the United States' main adversary during the Cold War (which lasted from the end of World War II to 1990). The Soviets began to sell arms to the revolutionary regime. Concerned about the regime's violations of human rights, as well as its ever-closer ties with the Soviets, the United States had already broken diplomatic relations with Cuba in January 1960 and had begun planning a series of attempts to overthrow Castro, all of which failed.

Canada, however, maintained full diplomatic and trade

relations with the Castro government, and has maintained them to this day. Since the start of the Cuban revolution, the successive administrations of the Canadian government have taken the stance that a policy of cooperation—as opposed to the American policy of confrontation—is best for the people of Cuba and Canada. Many Cuban exile groups have been critical of that policy, arguing that Canada is obligated to speak out more against the regime's human rights violations. But the exiles have also noted in recent years that the Canadian government has more often condemned the regime's offenses.

From Dwight Eisenhower to George W. Bush, American presidents have consistently used policies designed to isolate Castro and Cuba. Early attempts to remove Castro depended greatly on the efforts of U.S.–based Cuban exiles who were trained by the Central Intelligence Agency (CIA). On April 17, 1961, some 1,500 armed men of Brigade 2506 landed at the Bay of Pigs, in the Zapata Swamp of south-central Cuba. One of the Castro government's first responses was to immediately jail as many as 100,000 people suspected of giving support to Brigade 2506 in Havana and other cities. The government also mobilized the army to surround the invaders on a small beachhead. Although the exiles had already begun a bombing campaign with some successful results, President John F. Kennedy, under pressure from the international community, decided against ordering additional air strikes that might have broken Castro's encirclement. Brigade 2506 was defeated after three days of fighting.

For those who opposed Castro, the defeat at the Bay of Pigs was yet one more setback in Cuba's long struggle for freedom. Not long thereafter, Castro officially declared that his revolution was communist, and that he himself was, in his words, "a Marxist-Leninist until the day I die." The United States responded to Castro's declaration and his general policies by imposing a trade embargo that remains to this day.

What many Cubans feared most had come true. Oppression was now practiced more in the open than ever. Political prisoners filled Cuba's jails, but they were not the only ones vulnerable to persecution. Simply not showing enthusiastic support for the government often meant the loss of a job or harassment by government-sponsored mobs. By 1962, nearly 200,000 Cubans had escaped the dictatorship, most of whom resettled in the United States.

The steady flow of migration was cut off, however, by the Cuban Missile Crisis of October 1962. That month U.S. satellite pictures showed that the Soviet Union was building nuclear missile sites in Cuba. President Kennedy demanded the sites be

(Right) Cuban militiamen and members of the Revolutionary Army celebrate their victory over the Cuban exiles.

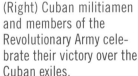

(Left) As U.S. president, John F. Kennedy maintained a policy of isolating Fidel Castro and Cuba. He also ordered the CIA to train Cuban exiles in the April 1961 Bay of Pigs Invasion, which ended in failure and was a major setback in the long campaign to end Castro's regime.

dismantled immediately and ordered a naval blockade of the island. For the next two weeks, the world found itself on the brink of nuclear war.

But the Soviets backed down. They dismantled the bases in exchange for a promise by the United States that it would not allow any more exile invasions of Cuba. In addition, direct flights between Cuba and the United States were brought to a halt, making it much more difficult for Castro's opponents to leave. It was not until 1965 that flights resumed. By then, Castro had secured a strong hold over the Cuban people. He organized Committees for the Defense of the Revolution in neighborhoods to spy on and harass those frustrated with the regime. Citizens were also required to "volunteer" on farms; those who did not show up to work were at risk of not having any employment.

A Communist Cuba

With the communization of Cuba, everyone worked for the government; even small retail shops—the pharmacy down the street, the corner bodega—had been taken over by the regime in what was called the "Great Revolutionary Offensive." Only the government was permitted to own businesses. As years went on, the regime maintained its restrictions and continued to send dissidents to jail, where conditions were terrible. The most famous political prisoners, called the *plantados* (roughly meaning "the ones who stood their ground"), lived for years in tiny cells, wearing nothing but their underwear and surviving on meager rations of rotten meat and spoiled beans.

The Cuban government's influence grew beyond the island during the 1960s. The Castro government sent advisors to instruct communist guerrillas fighting in the jungles and even in the cities of several Latin American countries. None of these revolutionary groups was able to take power except in Nicaragua, where a guerrilla group known as the Sandinistas ousted the dictator Anastasio Somoza and installed a socialist state modeled on Castro's Cuba. For most of the 1980s, the

Sandinistas were Cuba's principal ally in Latin America.

Cuban foreign influence extended even beyond the Americas. In the 1970s and 1980s, Castro sent troops overseas to fight alongside pro-communist rebels in Angola, Ethiopia, and other parts of Africa. He also sent military advisers to support the government in Nicaragua when a group of U.S.–backed anti-Sandinista guerrillas known as the contras rose in arms.

Despite Cuba's growing international influence, however, economic troubles plagued the country. There were food shortages, which some say were due to the U.S. embargo while others say were more likely due to the Castro government's mismanagement of agriculture and manufacturing. Whatever the case, nearly all consumer items—from clothing to soap to basic food staples—were rationed. Every Cuban family was issued a ration book that severely limited how much it could buy each month. This rationing system remains in operation today.

The Debate over Cuba

Cubans refugees cite the human rights abuses of Castro's regime as among their main reasons to flee the country. Many American and Canadian advocacy organizations for Cubans have supported the claims of these refugees. Yet the Cuban government has its defenders, both within and beyond the country's borders.

Castro's supporters say that after the revolution in 1959, Cuba set up free health care clinics, built new housing, and organized literacy campaigns to help more citizens read. Today, Cuba ranks among the leading countries in Latin America in terms of literacy rates and low infant mortality.

The counterargument Castro's critics make is that Cuba had already been among the region's most advanced countries *before* the president's takeover. They point out that by the 1940s and 1950s, Cuba ranked among the top three or four countries in Latin America in terms of literacy rate, infant mortality rate, and ownership of cars, telephones, and television sets. They also call attention to countries such as Costa Rica and Uruguay, small nations that remained among the most advanced in Latin America without removing all political freedoms like Cuba did.

The Refugee Crises

The lack of personal freedom, combined with the shortages of consumer goods, made many Cubans eager as ever to leave the country. In April 1980, in response to an incident involving asylum seekers at the Peruvian embassy in Havana, the Castro regime abruptly lifted restrictions on leaving the country. Over the next few months, more than 125,000 people left the island in boats and headed to Florida in what became known as the Mariel boatlift.

In the wake of the Mariel exodus, organizations such as Americas Watch, Amnesty International, and the United Nations Human Rights Commission began to issue reports covering the poor human rights conditions in Cuba. Their findings were a blow to the international prestige of Castro's regime.

Cuba's standing got worse in the late 1980s with the collapse of communism in Eastern Europe. Subsidies from the Soviet Union to Cuba were cut off after the communist system folded

A Cuban baby, one of the more than 125,000 refugees who participated in the Mariel boatlift of 1980, is lifted in the air in celebration of a safe arrival to Eglin Airforce Base, Florida. The refugees arrived over the course of six months, following Castro's sudden decision to lift restrictions on emigration.

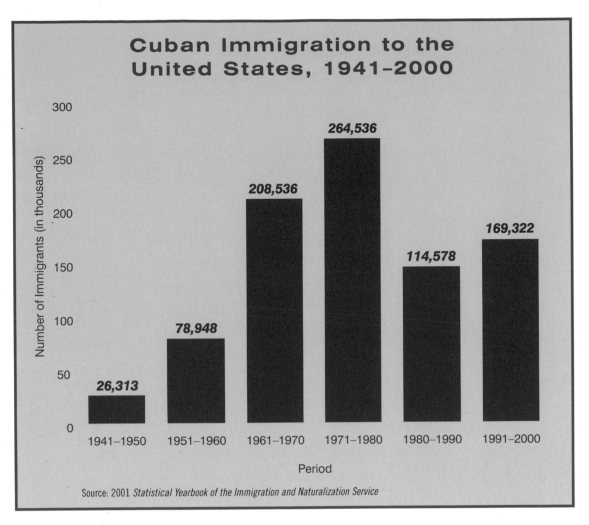

Cuban Immigration to the United States, 1941–2000

Number of Immigrants (in thousands)

Period	Number
1941–1950	26,313
1951–1960	78,948
1961–1970	208,536
1971–1980	264,536
1980–1990	114,578
1991–2000	169,322

Source: 2001 *Statistical Yearbook of the Immigration and Naturalization Service*

there, which put the national economy in even deeper trouble. The situation encouraged more Cubans, including the young generation who only knew life under Castro, to leave. In 1994 tens of thousands left Cuba in homemade rafts—an exodus that came to be known as the "rafter" crisis.

Because this major exodus was proof of the people's discontent, the Cuban government felt pressured to relax some of its stringent economic rules. It encouraged tourism from Western nations, legalized the use of U.S. currency (previously, Cubans were prosecuted for having American money), and permitted the operation of a number of privately owned businesses, most of which were tourist-related. But Cubans were angered that they were not permitted to enter the finest restaurants, resorts, and stores, which were reserved for foreigners who did not need rationing cards. And though the government's regulation of the economy was less rigid during this time, there was no move toward reforming Cuba's politically oppressive laws. New legislation passed in the early 1990s established even tougher penalties for criticizing the regime.

The next major crisis occurred in 1996 when Cuban air force jets shot down two civilian planes flown by members of Brothers to the Rescue, a Miami-based exile group that flew over the Florida straits looking for lost rafters. In response to the attacks, the U.S. government passed legislation that tightened the embargo and ensured that it would remain in place for some time.

Dissent and Policy Change

Also adding to the dissatisfaction of Cuban dissenters—and to their desire to leave—was the government's decision to ignore the advice of Pope John Paul II, which he offered during his January 1998 visit to Cuba. The first pope to visit Cuba called for "the world to open up to Cuba, and for Cuba to open up to the world." Despite the protests of international

Catholic Cubans receive communion from Pope John Paul II, who visited Cuba in January 1998. During his visit, the pope criticized the country's human rights abuses and also publicly called on international leaders to improve relations between Cuba and other countries.

leaders and activist organizations, dissidents who called for peaceful change in Cuba continued to be harassed, jailed, and fired from their jobs.

The persistence and frequency of Castro's repressive measures convinced Canada to reconsider its foreign policy with Cuba. Beginning in the late 1990s, the Canadian government acknowledged that its policy of engagement with Castro had not improved Cuba's human rights record after four decades, and it issued more criticisms of the Cuban government, in bilateral talks as well as in international forums. In addition, since the late 1990s, Canada has voted to censure Cuba at the annual UN Human Rights Commission meetings in Geneva. Nonetheless, Canada has not broken trade or diplomatic relations, and continues to speak out against the U.S. trade embargo.

In early 2002 one Cuban group led by activist Oswaldo Payá Sardiñas challenged the legitimacy of the government by collecting petition signatures. The document asked that the Cuban government restore the basics of democracy, such as multi-party elections, the release of political prisoners, freedom of speech, and freedom of the press. The regime responded by rejecting such changes, explaining that Cuba's socialist system was "untouchable." Later that year Payá was awarded the European Parliament's 2002 Sakharov Prize for Freedom of Thought. By early 2003 he had become an anti-Castro leader recognized the world over and remained committed to the pro-democracy struggle on the island.

But the human rights situation in Cuba still had not improved. In 2003, the Cuban government arrested and handed down long prison sentences to dozens of pro-democracy activists and supporters. The 2003 World Report issued by Human Rights Watch criticized the country's "lack of democracy and intolerance of domestic dissent" and the way its "government-controlled counts undermined the right to fair trial. . . ."

3 A History of Cuban Migration

Nearly one million Cubans have left their country for North America since the beginning of Castro's revolution in 1959, with the great majority moving to the United States. There have been many changes in immigration laws before and after the revolution, affecting Cubans as well as other immigrant groups. To have a good understanding of Cuban immigration, it is helpful to briefly examine the history of immigration to North America.

A Short History of U.S. Immigration

Immigration to the United States has been characterized by openness punctuated by periods of restriction. During the 17th, 18th, and 19th centuries, immigration was essentially open without restriction, and, at times, immigrants were even recruited to come to America. Between 1783 and 1820, approximately 250,000 immigrants arrived at U.S. shores. Between 1841 and 1860, more than 4 million immigrants came; most were from England, Ireland, and Germany.

Historically, race and ethnicity have played a role in legislation to restrict immigration. The Chinese Exclusion Act of 1882, which was not repealed until 1943, specifically prevented Chinese people from becoming U.S. citizens and did not allow Chinese laborers to immigrate for the next decade. An agreement with Japan in the early 1900s prevented most Japanese immigration to the United States.

◄For decades Cubans have attempted the often dangerous journey to Florida in all kinds of vessels—in this case, a 1951 Chevrolet truck. The makeshift boat was apprehended by the U.S. Coast Guard in July 2003. All 12 passengers were repatriated to Cuba.

Until the 1920s, no numerical restrictions on immigration existed in the United States, although health restrictions applied. The only other significant restrictions came in 1917, when passing a literacy test became a requirement for immigrants. Presidents Cleveland, Taft, and Wilson had vetoed similar measures earlier. In addition, in 1917 a prohibition was added to the law against the immigration of people from Asia (defined as the Asiatic barred zone). While a few of these prohibitions were lifted during World War II, they were not repealed until 1952, and even then Asians were only allowed in under very small annual quotas.

U.S. Immigration Policy from World War I to 1965

During World War I, the federal government required that all travelers to the United States obtain a visa at a U.S. consulate or diplomatic post abroad. As former State Department consular affairs officer C. D. Scully points out, by making that requirement permanent Congress, by 1924, established the framework of temporary, or non-immigrant visas (for study, work, or travel), and immigrant visas (for permanent residence). That framework remains in place today.

After World War I, cultural intolerance and bizarre racial theories led to new immigration restrictions. The House Judiciary Committee employed a eugenics consultant, Dr. Harry N. Laughlin, who asserted that certain races were inferior. Another leader of the eugenics movement, Madison Grant, argued that Jews, Italians, and others were inferior because of their supposedly different skull size.

The Immigration Act of 1924, preceded by the Temporary Quota Act of 1921, set new numerical limits on immigration based on "national origin." Taking effect in 1929, the 1924 act set annual quotas on immigrants that were specifically designed to keep out southern Europeans, such as Italians and Greeks. Generally no more than 100 people of the proscribed nationalities were permitted to immigrate.

While the new law was rigid, the U.S. Department of State's restrictive interpretation directed consular officers overseas to be even stricter in their application of the "public charge" provision. (A public charge is someone unable to support himself or his family.) As author Laura Fermi wrote, "In response to the new cry for restriction at the beginning of the [Great Depression] . . . the consuls were to interpret very strictly the clause prohibiting admission of aliens 'likely to become public charges; and to deny the visa to an applicant who in their opinion might become a public charge at any time.'"

In the early 1900s, more than one million immigrants a year came to the United States. In 1930—the first year of the national-origin quotas—approximately 241,700 immigrants were admitted. But under the State Department's strict interpretations, only 23,068 immigrants entered during 1933, the smallest total since 1831. Later these restrictions prevented many Jews in Germany and elsewhere in Europe from escaping what would become the Holocaust. At the height of the Holocaust in 1943, the United States admitted fewer than 6,000 refugees.

The Displaced Persons Act of 1948, the nation's first refugee law, allowed many refugees from World War II to settle in the United States. The law put into place policy changes that had already seen immigration rise from 38,119 in 1945 to 108,721 in 1946 (and later to 249,187 in 1950). One-third of those admitted between 1948 and 1951 were Poles, with ethnic Germans forming the second-largest group.

The 1952 Immigration and Nationality Act is best known for its restrictions against those who supported communism or anarchy. However, the bill's other provisions were quite restrictive and were passed over the veto of President Truman. The 1952 act retained the national-origin quota system for the Eastern Hemisphere. The Western Hemisphere continued to operate without a quota and relied on other qualitative factors to limit immigration. Moreover, during that time, the Mexican bracero program, from 1942 to 1964, allowed millions of

Mexican agricultural workers to work temporarily in the United States.

The 1952 act set aside half of each national quota to be divided among three preference categories for relatives of U.S. citizens and permanent residents. The other half went to aliens with high education or exceptional abilities. These quotas applied only to those from the Eastern Hemisphere.

A Halt to the National-Origin Quotas

The Immigration and Nationality Act of 1965 became a landmark in immigration legislation by specifically striking the racially based national-origin quotas. It removed the barriers to Asian immigration, which later led to opportunities to immigrate for many Filipinos, Chinese, Koreans, and others. The Western Hemisphere was designated a ceiling of 120,000 immigrants but without a preference system or per country limits.

In 1965 President Lyndon Johnson signed the Immigration and Nationality Act, inaugurating a new era of immigration. With the passage of the act, many foreign groups were able to immigrate to the United States in large numbers.

Modifications made in 1978 ultimately combined the Western and Eastern Hemispheres into one preference system and one ceiling of 290,000.

The 1965 act built on the existing system—without the national-origin quotas—and gave somewhat more priority to family relationships. It did not completely overturn the existing system but rather carried forward essentially intact the family immigration categories from the 1959 amendments to the Immigration and Nationality Act. Even though the text of the law prior to 1965 indicated that half of the immigration slots were reserved for skilled employment immigration, in practice, Immigration and Naturalization Service (INS) statistics show that 86 percent of the visas issued between 1952 and 1965 went for family immigration.

A number of significant pieces of legislation since 1980 have shaped the current U.S. immigration system. First, the Refugee Act of 1980 removed refugees from the annual world limit and established that the president would set the number of refugees who could be admitted each year after consultations with Congress.

Second, the 1986 Immigration Reform and Control Act (IRCA) introduced sanctions against employers who "knowingly" hired undocumented immigrants (those here illegally). It also provided amnesty for many undocumented immigrants.

Third, the Immigration Act of 1990 increased legal immigration by 40 percent. In particular, the act significantly increased the number of employment-based immigrants (to 140,000), while also boosting family immigration.

Fourth, the 1996 Illegal Immigration Reform and Immigrant Responsibility Act (IIRAIRA) significantly tightened rules that permitted undocumented immigrants to convert to legal status and made other changes that tightened immigration law in areas such as political asylum and deportation.

Fifth, in response to the September 11, 2001, terrorist attacks, the USA PATRIOT Act and the Enhanced Border Security and Visa Entry Reform Act tightened rules on the granting of visas to individuals from certain countries and enhanced the federal government's monitoring and detention authority over foreign nationals in the United States.

New U.S. Immigration Agencies

In a dramatic reorganization of the federal government, the Homeland Security Act of 2002 abolished the Immigration and Naturalization Service and transferred its immigration service and enforcement functions from the Department of Justice into a new Department of Homeland Security. The Customs Service, the Coast Guard, and parts of other agencies were also transferred into the new department.

The Department of Homeland Security, with regards to immigration, is organized as follows: The Bureau of Customs and Border Protection (BCBP) contains Customs and Immigration inspectors, who check the documents of travelers to the United States at air, sea, and land ports of entry; and Border Patrol agents, the uniformed agents who seek to prevent unlawful entry along the southern and northern border. The new Bureau of Immigration and Customs Enforcement (BICE) employs investigators, who attempt to find undocumented immigrants inside the United States, and Detention and Removal officers, who detain and seek to deport such individuals. The new Bureau of Citizenship and Immigration Services (BCIS) is where people go, or correspond with, to become U.S. citizens or obtain permission to work or extend their stay in the United States.

Following the terrorist attacks of September 11, 2001, the Department of Justice adopted several measures that did not require new legislation to be passed by Congress. Some of these measures created controversy and raised concerns about civil liberties. For example, FBI and INS agents detained for months more than 1,000 foreign nationals of Middle Eastern descent and refused to release the names of the individuals. It is alleged that the Department of Justice adopted tactics that discouraged the detainees from obtaining legal assistance. The Department

President Bush signs the Enhanced Border Security and Visa Entry Reform Act with congressional members in attendance, May 2002. The act, along with the USA PATRIOT Act, was passed in response to the September 2001 terrorist attacks.

of Justice also began requiring foreign nationals from primarily Muslim nations to be fingerprinted and questioned by immigration officers upon entry or if they have been living in the United States. Those involved in the September 11 attacks were not immigrants—people who become permanent residents with a right to stay in the United States—but holders of temporary visas, primarily visitor or tourist visas.

Immigration to the United States Today

Today, the annual rate of legal immigration is lower than that at earlier periods in U.S. history. For example, from 1901 to 1910 approximately 10.4 immigrants per 1,000 U.S. residents came to the United States. Today, the annual rate is about 3.5 immigrants per 1,000 U.S. residents. While the percentage of foreign-born people in the U.S. population has risen above 11 percent, it remains lower than the 13 percent or higher that prevailed in the country from 1860 to 1930. Still, as has been the case previously in U.S. history, some people argue that even legal immigration should be lowered. These people maintain that immigrants take jobs native-born Americans could fill and that U.S. population growth, which immigration contributes to, harms the environment. In 1996 Congress voted against efforts to reduce legal immigration.

Most immigrants (800,000 to one million annually) enter the United States legally. But over the years the undocumented (illegal) portion of the population has increased to about 2.8 percent of the U.S. population—approximately 8 million people in all.

Today, the legal immigration system in the United States contains many rules, permitting only individuals who fit into certain categories to immigrate—and in many cases only after waiting anywhere from 1 to 10 years or more, depending on the demand in that category. The system, representing a compromise among family, employment, and human rights concerns, has the following elements:

> A U.S. citizen may sponsor for immigration a spouse, parent, sibling, or minor or adult child.

> A lawful permanent resident (green card holder) may sponsor only a spouse or child.

> A foreign national may immigrate if he or she gains an employer sponsor.

> An individual who can show that he or she has a "well-founded fear of persecution" may come to the country as a refugee—or be allowed to stay as an asylee (someone who receives asylum).

Beyond these categories, essentially the only other way to immigrate is to apply for and receive one of the "diversity" visas, which are granted annually by lottery to those from "underrepresented" countries.

In 1996 changes to the law prohibited nearly all incoming immigrants from being eligible for federal public benefits, such as welfare, during their first five years in the country. Refugees were mostly excluded from these changes. In addition, families who sponsor relatives must sign an affidavit of support showing they can financially take care of an immigrant who falls on hard times.

A Short History of Canadian Immigration

In the 1800s, immigration into Canada was largely unrestricted. Farmers and artisans from England and Ireland made up a significant portion of 19th-century immigrants. England's Parliament passed laws that facilitated and encouraged the voyage to North America, particularly for the poor.

After the United States barred Chinese railroad workers from settling in the country, Canada encouraged the immigration of Chinese laborers to assist in the building of Canadian railways. Responding to the racial views of the time, the Canadian Parliament began charging a "head tax" for Chinese and South Asian (Indian) immigrants in 1885. The fee of $50—later raised to $500—was well beyond the means of laborers making one or two dollars a day. Later, the government sought additional ways to prohibit Asians from entering the country. For example, it decided to require a "continuous journey," meaning that immigrants to Canada had to travel from their country on a boat that made an uninterrupted passage. For immigrants or asylum seekers from Asia this was nearly impossible.

As the 20th century progressed, concerns about race led to further restrictions on immigration to Canada. These restrictions particularly hurt Jewish and other refugees seeking to flee persecution in Europe. Government statistics indicate that Canada accepted no more than 5,000 Jewish refugees before and during the Holocaust.

After World War II, Canada, like the United States, began accepting thousands of Europeans displaced by the war. Canada's laws were modified to accept these war refugees, as well as Hungarians fleeing Communist authorities after the crushing of the 1956 Hungarian Revolution.

The Immigration Act of 1952 in Canada allowed for a "tap

on, tap off" approach to immigration, granting administrative authorities the power to allow more immigrants into the country in good economic times, and fewer in times of recession. The shortcoming of such an approach is that there is little evidence immigrants harm a national economy and much evidence they contribute to economic growth, particularly in the growth of the labor force.

In 1966 the government of Prime Minister Lester Pearson introduced a policy statement stressing how immigrants were key to Canada's economic growth. With Canada's relatively small population base, it became clear that in the absence of newcomers, the country would not be able to grow. The policy was introduced four years after Parliament enacted important legislation that eliminated Canada's own version of racially based national-origin quotas.

In 1967 a new law established a points system that awarded entry to potential immigrants using criteria based primarily on an individual's age, language ability, skills, education, family relationships, and job prospects. The total points needed for entry of an immigrant is set by the Minister of Citizenship and Immigration Canada. The new law also estab-

Lester Pearson, prime minister of Canada from 1963 to 1968, believed that immigrants were key to the country's economic growth. In 1966 the Canadian government introduced a statement stressing the importance of an open immigration policy.

lished a category for humanitarian (refugee) entry.

The 1976 Immigration Act refined and expanded the possibility for entry under the points system, particularly for those seeking to sponsor family members. The act also expanded refugee and asylum law to comport with Canada's international obligations. The law established five basic categories for immigration into Canada: 1) family; 2) humanitarian; 3) independents (including skilled workers), who immigrate to Canada on their own; 4) assisted relatives; and 5) business immigrants (including investors, entrepreneurs, and the self-employed).

The new Immigration and Refugee Protection Act, which took effect June 28, 2002, made a series of modifications to existing Canadian immigration law. The act, and the regulations that followed, toughened rules on those seeking asylum and the process for removing people unlawfully in Canada.

The law modified the points system, adding greater flexibility for skilled immigrants and temporary workers to become permanent residents, and evaluating skilled workers on the weight of their transferable skills as well as those of their specific occupation. The legislation also made it easier for employers to have a labor shortage declared in an industry or sector, which would facilitate the entry of foreign workers in that industry or sector.

On family immigration, the act permitted parents to sponsor dependent children up to the age of 22 (previously 19 was the maximum age at which a child could be sponsored for immigration). The act also allowed partners in common-law arrangements, including same-sex partners, to be considered as family members for the purpose of immigration sponsorship. Along with these liberalizing measures, the act also included provisions to address perceived gaps in immigration-law enforcement.

Cubans in the United States

The 2000 U.S. Census estimated that there were 1.2 million Cubans in the United States, a figure that includes exiles, their

American–born descendants, as well as Cuban Americans whose families had settled there before the Castro revolution. The Cuban presence in the United States is four centuries old. Although the vast majority of Cubans came after Fidel Castro took power, Cubans lived there before the land known as America became the United States.

Cubans lived in Florida when it was a colony of Spain, from the 1500s to 1821. In that year, the territory of Florida was sold to the United States, then still a young nation. Many Cubans made their home in St. Augustine, the oldest European settlement in what is now the United States. The settlement's imposing fortress, Castillo San Marcos, was designed by a Cuban engineer named Ignacio Daza and constructed under the direction of Laureano Torres de Ayala, one of the three Cuban-born governors in Spanish Florida's history. A garrison of troops defended its 12-foot walls, and with the help of an armada that sailed from Havana under the Cuban-born general Esteban Berroa, it turned back a British attempt to conquer St. Augustine in 1702. A second attack in 1740 also failed.

Cubans were active during the American Revolutionary War as well. In 1779 Cuban troops under Spanish field marshal Bernardo de Gálvez forced the British out of a line of forts that stretched along the Gulf of Mexico. Two years later, Gálvez and his troops reconquered Pensacola, Florida, with the help of yet another armada from Havana led by the Cuban Juan Manuel de Cagigal. The victory meant redcoats were pinned down who would have otherwise been mobilized against the Continental army in Virginia at the Battle of Yorktown. These soldiers' absence made even more certain the British defeat in the war's final battle.

Cubans played a key role in that decisive battle as well. With the Continental army running out of money and on the verge of mutiny, George Washington asked French Admiral DeGrasse for help. De Grasse sailed to Havana and with the help of Cagigal—the new governor of Cuba—convinced residents of Havana to donate an estimated 1.2 million French livres to

Washington's army. It was enough to supply troops with the weapons, munitions, and uniforms they needed to defeat the British.

The 19th century brought a change in Cuba's self-image as well as in its attitude toward the United States. In the preceding century, Cubans had helped the United States gain independence from Great Britain; now, inspired by the American Revolution, Cubans sought help from the United States to gain their own independence from Spain. In the first decades of the 19th century, there were armed uprisings as well as peaceful attempts at political reform, but all of them failed, as Spanish authorities cracked down on dissenters. Beginning in the 1820s, Cubans fleeing this political repression started to arrive in America.

Some exiles went to Key West, Florida where by 1831 there was a Cuban-owned cigar factory in operation. New Orleans, too, had a small Cuban community. But most Cubans of the period settled in New York City, where for several decades they

An 18th-century engraving of St. Augustine, Florida, the oldest European settlement in America. Many Cubans had lived in the colony of Florida before the Spanish sold it to the United States in 1821.

organized to fight for Cuban independence. The best-known leader of the period was Narciso López. In 1848 he established contacts with pro-slavery American Southerners who hoped to take Cuba from Spain and annex it as a slave state. They helped finance an expedition led by López in 1850. The expedition went from Florida to Cuba with 600 armed Cuban exiles and American soldiers. López and his men took the town of Cárdenas and held it for one day, until Spanish troops counterattacked and forced them to sail back to Florida. He led a second expedition the following year, but was captured and executed by Spanish authorities.

Exiles continued to orchestrate an independence movement in the United States well into the 1870s, as the Ten Years War raged in Cuba. The rebels even had representatives who asked the administration of President Ulysses S. Grant for help in the war against Spain. The representatives were turned down, but nevertheless, Cubans kept coming to America.

As years passed, the Cuban community in New York grew large enough to form small but well-established neighborhoods

The flag of Cuba was created by independence leader Narcisco López in 1849. Its horizontal stripes and color pattern was inspired by the design of the U.S. flag.

in the Lower East Side. There were Cuban restaurants, newspapers, bodegas, and at least one Cuban-owned Spanish-language bookstore. Around the same period, the small community in Key West grew as large as the one in New York. In 1875, the city even elected a Cuban American mayor, and in the 1880s, it sent two representatives to Florida's state legislature. A decade later Cuban cigar manufacturers founded Ybor City, the oldest neighborhood in what is now Tampa.

Cubans living in America had a pivotal role in waging the 1895 War of Independence. The revolution was led by José Martí, a poet and a national hero. Martí arrived in New York City in 1880 after being deported from Cuba for his pro-independence activities. While living in New York, he wrote some of his most famous poems and also worked as an art critic for the *New York Sun*.

But the struggle for an independent Cuba was Martí's principal motivation. When he first arrived to New York he found a Cuban community still sore from defeat in the Ten Years War, which had ended two years earlier. He organized rallies throughout Manhattan, renewing the call to independence and urging fellow exiles to unite. The speeches he delivered have become famous in Cuban history.

Martí's pro-independence activities continued for a decade. In 1891 he first visited the booming communities of Key West and Tampa, home to perhaps 10,000 Cubans. The locals welcomed him as a hero, as the great hope for a free Cuba. His next years were spent traveling between New York and Florida to raise funds, buy arms, recruit troops, and organize the leadership for a new rebellion. When everything was ready, he gave the order and Cuba's War of Independence began on February 24, 1895. Martí landed in Cuba that April, but was killed in battle five weeks later.

Republican Years

Cuba won independence from Spain in 1898 and was granted sovereignty from the U.S. administration in 1902. In its formative period as a republic, Cuba suffered through corrupt governments that were hard-pressed to revitalize a country beset by years of warfare. Cubans continued to come to the United States. Until Gerardo Machado became dictator in 1925, Cubans coming to America were primarily seeking economic opportunities. During the Machado dictatorship, however, the motivation was more political—civilians were fleeing persecution and a number of leaders were fleeing to a safe place where they could plan their next move. President Mario García Menocal and future president Carlos Mendieta were among those who lived temporarily in the United States while plotting the overthrow of Machado, which took place in 1933.

During the two decades after Machado's removal from office and the return to stability in Cuba, the motivation behind Cuban migration to the United States was mainly economic. But political repression began to once again drive Cubans out with the reemergence of Fulgencio Batista in 1952. This former army sergeant had been the country's behind-the-scenes ruler during the 1930s. When he overthrew elected president Carlos Prío in 1952, he initiated another period of corruption and misrule.

Throughout the rest of the 1950s, Cuban leaders in the United States resumed the tradition of plotting to overthrow tyranny in the homeland. Prío was arrested by federal authorities on charges of conspiracy to smuggle arms, and a young man named Fidel Castro traveled to Cuban communities along the east coast, raising funds to arm his own anti-Batista group. Prío agreed to meet Castro at a secret meeting in Texas in 1956, and provided enough funds for an armed landing in December.

It was with that landing that Castro and his group began the fight that ended with Batista's fall in 1959. The government Castro established soon became dictatorial too, which brought about the first mass Cuban exodus to America. As had happened during the Spanish colonial period, the Machado years of the 1930s, and the Batista dictatorship, Cubans were impelled to flee to America, where once again exile leaders plotted to overthrow the current dictator.

By the time of the Castro administration, the idea of seeking freedom in the United States was already a familiar one to many. The difference between this period of migration and previous ones was that under Castro, thousands more made the trip, and had arrived in their new land to settle for good.

The Castro Years and the Golden Exiles

The exiles of the Castro era have come in four different waves, each one with a distinct profile characterized by its education, social class, and race. The first wave to come was called the "Golden Exiles." They were mostly members of Cuba's pre-Castro elite and its educated middle class, and arrived between the beginning of the revolution and the mid-1960s.

Father Varela and the Early Cuban Americans

One of the most famous of the early Cubans in America was Félix Varela, a philosopher and Catholic priest who founded *El Habanero*, a pro-independence, anti-slavery newspaper. It was the first regularly issued Spanish-language publication in the United States.

The Cuban independence movement in America struggled to find a single cause that everyone could support. Some exiles sought outright independence for Cuba, others preferred to remain a part of the Spanish empire but with more self-rule, and a third group wanted Cuba to become a U.S. state. Father Varela grew frustrated with the bickering of various factions and with Spain's unwillingness to accept reform of any kind, and so he decided to shift his attention toward his priestly duties.

Varela founded a school for children of the poverty-stricken Irish immigrants who lived in Manhattan's most infamous 19th-century slum, the Five Corners. During the cholera epidemic of 1832, he set up a medical center for victims whom hospitals were wary to treat. His dedication to the immigrants earned him the title "the Vicar of the Irish." Varela died in 1848. A U.S. postage stamp in his honor was issued in 1997.

The dictatorship of Fulgencia Batista during the 1950s marked a difficult period of government corruption and misrule for Cuba, and initiated another wave of Cuban exiles looking to escape political repression.

The next wave included passengers of what were known as the Freedom Flights, which ran between 1965 and 1973. Many individuals of this wave were small-business owners, factory workers, or farmers. The next major group arrived in a period of just five months in 1980, during the Mariel boatlift. They were largely working-class people, but some of the exiles were the first professionals educated under the Castro regime to migrate. There were more non-white Cubans among the Marielitos than in previous waves. The fourth and most recent wave began in 1994 with the "rafter" crisis, and is largely made up of young men and women who were born after 1959 and have lived their entire lives under Castro's rule.

People with ties to the Batista regime were the first to leave after the Rebel Army had driven them out and put Castro into power on January 1, 1959. Some 3,000 government officials, soldiers, policemen, and business people with links to the old dictatorship fled the island during the first few weeks of that year. The regime they served was so unpopular that the vast majority of Cubans were happy to see them leave.

But it did not take long for a group of Cubans who had supported Castro in the revolution to become disenchanted with the system he was working to establish. After the revolutionary government began to curb freedoms and nationalize businesses, the educated elite decided conditions were so intolerable they had to leave.

Nearly 260,000 of the Golden Exiles left between 1959 and 1962. An overwhelming number of these immigrants were Cuba's leading men and women in the professional and business sectors. A study undertaken in 1963 by Stanford University found that 7.8 percent of the Golden Exiles had been lawyers, while the most recent census prior to the study, taken in 1953, reported that lawyers comprised only 0.5 percent of Cuba's population. Another 34 percent of the group were classed as "professional or managerial," compared to 9 percent of Cuba's population. And more than a third had a high school or college degree, compared to 4 percent of all Cubans.

The education and high income of these Cuban newcomers made them different from many immigrants who had come to the United States in decades past. In the 19th century, the majority of those who left Poland, Italy, Ireland, Germany, and other countries were driven by economic motives, hoping that in the United States they could find work opportunities that were difficult to find back home. Cubans, on the other hand, left their country primarily for political reasons. They preferred to be thought of as "exiles" or "refugees" and not "immigrants" because the former terms conveyed that they had indeed fled political repression. Nestor Carbonell, an exile of this wave who later became an executive at Pepsi-Cola, wrote of the Golden Exiles: "We did not come as immigrants pulled by the American economic dream, but as refugees pushed by the Cuban political nightmare."

What motivated many exiles during these early years was not the traditional immigrant desire to rebuild lives in a new country, but a zeal to overthrow the dictatorship that ruled their beloved homeland. And because they believed ousting Castro would take a short time, they expected they would live in America only temporarily and would return to Cuba after Castro's removal. Consequently, in the beginning they paid less attention to rebuilding shattered careers or reestablishing lost businesses than to fighting the regime in Havana. Soon many anti-Castro groups—some of whom were rivals—sprang up.

Among the Golden Exiles was a military group that with U.S. assistance launched the failed Bay of Pigs invasion. It was by far the largest and best-known anti-Castro operation.

Throughout late 1961 and into 1962, exile groups conducted hit-and-run guerrilla operations against military targets in Cuba. The agenda of the Golden Exiles was disrupted in 1962 with the Missile Crisis in October. The United States discovered that the Soviet Union was installing nuclear missiles in Cuba. President Kennedy demanded their removal, and the Soviets backed down, avoiding a possible nuclear war.

But the end of the crisis brought repercussions for the Cuban exiles. An agreement between the U.S. and Soviet governments stated that no more exile raids on Cuba would be launched from American soil. It also stated that all direct scheduled flights between Cuba and the United States would end. From that point on any Cuban who wanted to leave would have to first ask permission to go to a third country—most often, Spain or Mexico—and there ask the federal government for a visa to enter the United States.

This dramatically slowed the flow of Cubans to America. Only about 15,000 arrived in 1963, and the same number arrived in 1964, compared to the more than 75,000 who arrived in the first nine months of 1962, before the October missile crisis. Some of the new exiles did come via a third country, but it was hard for them to acquire permission from the government. Many Cubans who could not get permission decided to escape illegally, crossing the dangerous Florida Straits in boats or rafts made of inner tubes. Tens of thousands more would do the same in the coming years.

Soon enough discontent built up in Cuba, and Castro decided to finally give potential defectors the opportunity to leave voluntarily. In late September 1965, he declared that the northern port of Camarioca would be open to anyone who wanted to make the crossing to the United States.

Freedom Flights

In the weeks following Castro's decision to open Camarioca, Cubans in Miami rented just about anything that could float and headed to the port to bring waiting relatives to the United States. Nearly 5,000 arrived in all manner of seacraft—leaky sailboats, trawlers, tugboats. The exodus became so chaotic that the Castro and American governments negotiated for the resumption of flights to the United States. The decision marked the beginning of the Vuelos de la Libertad (Freedom Flights).

Although the Castro government allowed the flights, it also placed restrictions on who was permitted to leave. Several categories of skilled workers and professionals deemed essential to Cuba had to remain in the country. Those who could apply to leave had their property confiscated and were forced to spend months working on farms while waiting their turn to fly out of the country.

The Freedom Flights began in December 1965 and ended in April 1973. Approximately 250,000 Cubans flew to America during those years, and by the end of the period, the Cuban-born population of the United States had grown to more than half a million.

Because of the occupation-based restrictions Castro put in place for this second wave of exiles, the group was in many ways different from the Golden Exiles. A large segment consisted of small-business owners, factory workers, and farmers. Only 12 percent had jobs described as "professional or managerial," compared to 34 percent among Golden Exiles. In a 1980 study, 57 percent of Freedom Flights arrivals were said to be "blue collar, service or agricultural workers."

Upon their arrival in Miami, the exiles were housed in temporary barracks near the airport nicknamed Casas de la Libertad (Houses of Liberty). Under a resettlement program established by the U.S. government, thousands went to live in states as far away as Alaska and Wyoming—in many ways, worlds removed from the Cuban neighborhoods of South Florida. But most found their way back to Miami or moved to Union City and West New York, towns in New Jersey that by that point had a large Cuban population.

In the 1960s and 1970s, the attorney general's authority to "parole" people into the United States allowed Cubans to stay lawfully in the United States. However, granting parole status to Cubans did not guarantee permanent residence (the right to

The Peter Pan Kids

Shortly after taking power, the Castro regime instituted programs in schools that would indoctrinate children with regime dogma and philosophy. A number of parents feared that they would lose their parental rights, and subsequently, their ties with their songs and daughters. They made a heartbreaking decision: to send the children unaccompanied by their parents to the United States to escape the Castro regime.

From late 1960 until 1962, some 14,000 Cuban youngsters fled to America in what became known as Operation Peter Pan. The Catholic Archdiocese of Miami organized the operation, with help from Castro opponents in Cuba. Children who escaped first stayed in camps in South Florida; from there, some moved in with relatives. Others ended up with strangers who volunteered to take them in.

When the Missile Crisis of 1962 ended all flights from Cuba to the United States, Operation Peter Pan ended, too. For the kids who had made it to the United States, it was very difficult knowing they might not see their parents again. Most families eventually reunited, however. When the Freedom Flights began in December 1965, the parents of the Peter Pan children were given priority. Some 5,000 families were reunited within the first six months of the Freedom Flights.

stay permanently). The Cuban Adjustment Act, passed in 1966, was a crucial piece of legislation that has since guided much of U.S. policy towards Cuban refugees. The act allows Cubans, regardless of how they arrive, to become permanent residents (green card holders) after being physically present in the United States for one year or more. Between 1946 and 1998, approximately 618,000 Cubans adjusted to permanent residence, according to the Congressional Research Service.

President Lyndon B. Johnson signed the Cuban Adjustment Act while standing in front of the Statue of Liberty, a symbol of America's open policy toward immigrants and refugees. "I declare this afternoon to the people of Cuba that those who seek refuge here in America will find it," he said. "The dedication of America to our traditions as an asylum for the oppressed is going to be upheld."

This new law recognized the reality that most arriving Cubans were not going to live in the United States temporarily, as the Golden Exiles had believed they would upon their arrival in the early 1960s. The law was also a reminder to Cubans that seven years had passed since the Castro takeover, and that ousting him could not be accomplished as quickly as they once believed. Although many did not completely forget about organizing a resistance against the dictatorship, they did begin to focus more on resettling and rebuilding their lives and careers in their new land.

The existence of the Cuban Adjustment Act helps explains much of the distinction between how Haitian and Cuban refugees have been treated since 1966, as well as the reason why even today Cubans are generally not detained for long periods of time after arriving in the United States. Because Cubans are eligible to become permanent residents in the United States upon their arrival, it makes little sense to use taxpayer dollars on keeping the individuals detained for a year, simply for them to be released after that period.

In contrast, the Haitians have received an altogether different kind of treatment from the U.S. government and the immigration departments. In a controversial policy decision that went into effect at the end of 2001, the administration of George W. Bush started to detain almost all Haitians who made it to U.S. soil via boat. This affected in particular the more than 200 Haitian men, women, and children who ran aground at Key Biscayne, Florida, on a 50-foot boat in October 2002. Attorney General John Ashcroft argued that the policy was necessary to prevent a "mass migration" of Haitians, and in the spring of 2003 invoked "national security" to justify the continuing detention of Haitians fleeing to the United States. (This policy meant that rather than being let out on bond while their asylum claims before immigration judges were being decided, Haitians would remain detained for nine months or more.)

Mariel

Relatively few Cubans arrived in the first years after the Freedom Flights ended in 1973. In 1979, just 2,644 made their way to the United States, the fewest since the start of the revolution. But the following year, over 125,000 Cubans arrived in the space of just five months. This third major exodus was the Mariel boatlift, which was sparked by the actions of 12 Cubans from Havana. On April 1, 1980, the group commandeered a bus and crashed the gates of the Peruvian embassy, hoping to take advantage of a Latin American diplomatic custom that recognizes embassies as places of refuge for those fleeing repression.

When word got out that the group of 12 had successfully defected, thousands headed to the Peruvian embassy to seek asylum, too. Looking to dump the burden entirely on Peru, the Castro government removed its security detail, and soon 10,800 Cuban crowded the embassy compound. Peru granted all of them asylum, but then the Castro regime, embarrassed at the spectacle of so many citizens wanting to leave, sealed off the neighborhood and allowed no one to leave.

The embassy was, of course, not prepared to house, feed, and provide bathrooms for nearly 11,000 people. Conditions in the compound became terrible. People slept on the ground, went hungry, and lived in filth. Facing pressure from the international community and its own people, the Castro government finally decided to allow the people in the embassy to exit the country. What's more, it opened the port of Mariel to anyone who wanted to leave. Just as in the opening of Camarioca 15 years earlier, thousands of Cubans took advantage of the opportunity.

However, the scale of the Mariel exodus was much bigger than that of the Camarioca boatlift. By the middle of May, 3,000 Cubans were arriving in South Florida every day. On the peak day, June 3, no less than 6,000 Cubans landed—a larger total than that of the entire Camarioca boatlift.

But the flood turned into a trickle in August when the U.S. Navy and Coast Guard began to turn back boats that were leaving South Florida to pick up relatives in Mariel. All activity

A boat full of Cuban refugees arrives in Key West, Florida, as part of the massive Mariel boatlift of 1980. The state government of Florida was challenged to handle the sudden influx of more than 125,000 refugees.

ended when the Cuban government shut down the port of Mariel on September 25. By that date, 125,266 Cubans had made it to freedom since the boatlift began.

The exiles of this third wave differed in many ways from those of previous waves. There were many more non-whites—estimated totals of this group in the boatlift range from 15 to 40 percent, at a time when perhaps 95 percent of Cubans in America were white. Also, a larger segment of this exile group were writers, musicians, painters, and other artists who no longer wanted to endure the restrictions on freedom of expression imposed in Cuba.

Most Marielitos were blue-collar workers, unlike the majority of the Golden Exiles, who were professionals. In this respect the Marielitos had more in common with the people who left on the Freedom Flights. Yet there was one important difference between the two groups: the exiles of the Freedom Flights included many people who had once owned small businesses and had entrepreneurial skills that they quickly put to use in the United States, while most Mariel refugees—a majority of whom were young men—had grown up under a communist economy that banned private businesses. Relatively few of them had entrepreneurial skills.

The Mariel boatlift was a tremendous shock to the state of Florida, as the Miami community suddenly had to deal with 125,000 new arrivals. It was faced with many new challenges: Where would these immigrants find housing and jobs? Where would these new students, totaling more than 12,000, find room in local schools?

While the exodus increased the labor force in the Miami area by 7 percent over this short period, a January 1990 study in *Industrial and Labor Relations Review* by Princeton University economist David Card found that the Marielitos did not disrupt the city's employment figures. "The Mariel immigration had essentially no effect on the wages or employment outcomes of non-Cuban workers in the Miami labor market," Card wrote. "And, perhaps even more surprising, the Mariel immigration had no strong effect on the wages of other Cubans." What Card observed, as many economists have also found, is that while immigrants fill jobs, they also create jobs through consumer spending, investment, and starting businesses.

At first, refugees were temporarily housed in emergency shelters such as churches and gymnasiums. When these buildings were filled, officials placed refugees in improvised places like Miami's Orange Bowl Stadium and established a gigantic "Tent City" under a highway overpass near the Little Havana neighborhood. Later the refugees were transferred to processing centers in Key West, Tamiami Park, Opa Locka, and the Krome Detention Center near the marshes of the Everglades. There the refugees were fingerprinted, photographed, given medical tests, and questioned to make certain they were not spies or criminals.

Immigration officials released those exiles with sponsors who guaranteed they would not become a public charge. Some 60,000 who did not find sponsors were sent to camps in four military bases: Eglin Air Force Base, on the Florida Panhandle; Fort Chaffee, Arkansas; Fort Indiantown Gap, Pennsylvania; and Fort McCoy, Wisconsin. The camps were beset by violence committed by some of the criminals Castro had let loose, as well as riots that broke out at the Chaffee and Indiantown forts.

Owing to Castro's willingness to get rid of certain undesirable elements in Cuba, a number of the arrivals were criminals and mental hospital patients. Cuban officials had opened a number of the country's jails and mental hospitals and put the inmates onto the Mariel boats. A U.S. House Appropriations Committee report found that approximately 10 percent of the Mariel Cubans may have possessed a mental illness or criminal background that would have made them ineligible to enter the United States under the law.

Eventually, many of the worst Cuban criminals ended up in prison. Those in the refugee camps with no criminal record were released. Within 10 years, the Mariel generation reached a level of success similar to that of earlier waves of Cubans and had become a part of the community in South Florida.

The Rafters

The next major wave of Cubans to arrive in America was set off by yet another crisis. Just before dawn on July 3, 1994, the Cuban coast guard stopped an old tugboat, nicknamed *13 de Marzo*, that was carrying 72 Cuban exiles who hoped to make it to the United States. The boat was stopped at sea just 7 miles (11 kilometers) from Havana.

The government vessels rammed the *13 de Marzo* to make it sink, then sprayed the deck with high-pressure water hoses that sent people flying into the water and ripped babies from their mothers' arms. A total of 41 people drowned. The survivors were arrested on charges of attempting to leave the country illegally.

The Castro government called it an accident, but many Cuban citizens were not convinced that it was. Some dissenting Cubans began wearing black armbands in mourning. Protests became louder in August of that year, when 30,000 people took to the streets of Havana in the largest anti-government demonstration since Castro took power. Scores of protesters were arrested. Two years later, the Inter-American Commission on Human Rights supported the protesters' claims with a report concluding that the government was responsible for the massacre of innocent passengers aboard the *13 de Marzo*.

Tensions between the government and the people remained high. In late summer of 1994, in an attempt to rid Cuba of the protester element, Castro once again ordered security forces to allow people to leave. In just a few weeks, some 32,000 Cubans made it to the United States. People were so desperate to leave they used almost anything that could float—inner tubes from tires, pieces of Styrofoam, plywood planks. Out at sea, refugees suffered sunburn, exposure, and dehydration. Some experts estimate that thousands drowned during the trek.

A primary difference between the rafters (or *balseros*, as they

Cuban American demonstrators protest the Clinton administration's response to the rafter crisis of 1994. For the first time since 1959, Cuban refugees picked up at sea were not immediately brought into the United States; they were instead detained at the U.S. Navy base at Guantánamo Bay, Cuba.

were called in Spanish) and earlier Cuban refugees was that the majority of rafters were too young to remember life in Cuba before Castro. They were truly the children of the revolution, and they had left behind the only life they knew. Another major difference was in the way the U.S. government received this group. Fearing another Mariel crisis, the administration of President Bill Clinton ruled that the rafters would not be allowed to immediately enter the country. It was a landmark decision: for the first time since 1959, Cuban refugees were not permitted automatic entry to the United States.

The government did not send the rafters directly back to Cuba, however. Until a decision was made about how to handle the rafters, they would be held in a camp at Guantánamo, a naval base that the U.S. had controlled since 1902. Over the first few months about a third of the 30,000 rafters at

Guantánamo were granted entry to the United States on a case-by-case basis.

Their arrival was not a shock for the South Florida community as Mariel had been. The total of 30,000 refugees for this exodus was much lower than the 125,000 of Mariel, and Miami was more prepared to receive refugees this time. The Cuban community was more politically influential, much wealthier, and more integrated with the Miami establishment than it was in 1980. All these factors meant that newcomers could more easily find jobs, housing, and education. Civic organizations such as the Cuban American National Council set up schools for children who had difficulty making the transition. Another group, the Cuban American National Foundation, provided employment and temporary health insurance benefits to a number of the refugees.

On September 9, 1994, the United States and Cuba signed an agreement whereby the U.S. would take Cubans it interdicted

U.S. security personnel lead a Cuban immigrant off a bus at the Guantánamo base in June 1995. In May of that year, the United States and Cuba signed an agreement stating that U.S. immigration authorities would bring more Cuban rafters to Guantánamo Bay and no longer automatically grant them asylum.

at sea to a "safe haven" outside of the United States, rather than letting them onto the mainland as they had before. In return, Cuba would actively discourage its citizens from sailing to America. The U.S. government also agreed to admit through legal channels a minimum of 20,000 Cuban immigrants a year in addition to the immediate relatives of Cubans who had become U.S. citizens. The government has implemented this commitment primarily through lotteries of eligible Cuban citizens who wish to migrate. (More than 400,000 people participated in these lotteries, an indication of how widespread the desire is to leave Cuba and come to America.)

On May 2, 1995, the United States signed a second agreement with the Castro government that paved the way for the admission of more Cubans housed at Guantánamo. Following this agreement, the United States began sending additional Cubans interdicted at sea directly back to Cuba, rather than to a third country. In exchange, Cuba made a promise to not take retaliatory action against the returnees.

By the end of May, the remaining rafters had been given permission to finally enter America. The United States, as part of its agreement with Cuba, had made it an official policy to no longer grant automatic asylum to Cubans fleeing Castro. In what has become known as the "wet foot/dry foot" policy, rafters caught at sea by U.S. authorities were sent back to Cuba, but those who made it to the U.S. shore would be allowed to stay.

As of this writing, there has not been another mass exodus of Cubans to the United States since the May 1995 agreement between the two governments. Some migrants arrive through the regular immigration process; others continue to depart in rafts or larger boats, albeit in smaller numbers and with the knowledge that the U.S. Coast Guard can intercept them at sea and send them back to Cuba. However, if those fleeing Cuba are intercepted they have a chance to express a fear of persecution and can still receive asylum if their cases are convincing and meet the official definition of a refugee.

Cubans in Canada

The historic ties between Canada and Cuba are weaker than those between the United States and Cuba, and as a result, Canada has not been a traditional destination for Cubans escaping either the Castro dictatorship or any of the repressive regimes that preceded it. Another decisive factor working against Cuban immigration to Canada is the great distance between the two countries, which would never facilitate a boatlift to Canada such as the Mariel boatlift or the "rafter" exodus of the 1990s.

A live news image via the CNN network shows three Cuban refugees refusing to be rescued, May 2003. Many Cuban rafters evade rescue attempts because they know that under the U.S. "wet foot/dry foot" policy, they will be sent back to Cuba if they board a U.S. vessel at sea. If, however, they reach U.S. shores unassisted, they can be permitted to stay.

Still, though their numbers are relatively low, some Cuban exiles have resettled in Canada. They enter the country through two ways—either as immigrants or as political refugees. Those entering as immigrants must first get an exit visa from the Cuban government, just as they must do to resettle in the United States or any other country. They must also meet the requirements of Canada's immigration laws, meaning they would likely have to qualify under the Canadian points system or be eligible for entry on humanitarian grounds.

Until recently, Cubans had complained that legitimate asylum applicants were too often denied asylum and then deported. They argued that the Canadian government's friendly relations with the Castro regime kept immigration authorities from really seeing the persecution that Cubans faced. But there have been fewer complaints since the late 1990s. During those years, coinciding with a new Canadian foreign policy that was more openly critical of the Castro government, Canadian immigration authorities began to give more credibility to Cubans' fears of persecution. As a result, more defectors have been permitted to stay. Refugee advocates estimate that 4,500 Cubans have been granted asylum in Canada between 1998 and mid-2003.

During the years, small groups of visiting Cuban athletes and musicians were granted asylum. One of the most well-known cases of group defection occurred in the summer of 2002, when 22 members of a Cuban Catholic youth group defected while in Toronto for a church service given by Pope John Paul II. They were sheltered in safe houses by the Cuban Canadian Foundation and eventually given asylum as political refugees.

4 NEW AMERICAN LIVES

The first wave of Cubans to arrive in the United States after the 1959 revolution generally worried less about resettling than had the many millions of immigrants arriving before and after them. Unlike other immigrant groups, these Cuban exiles believed they would be living only temporarily in the United States. They had planned that once Castro's regime had fallen, they would return to Cuba.

These Cuban exiles contributed most of their planning and resources toward the Bay of Pigs invasion. The failure of the invasion was a huge setback for anti-Castro exiles. Smaller hit-and-run guerrilla operations continued after Bay of Pigs, though without the valued support of the United States. The exiles stuck to the belief that the Castro regime would soon fall from power, but by the mid-1960s major developments had dashed their hopes: there was Castro's new alliance with the Soviet Union, which gave the regime support from a formidable superpower; and there was the prohibition of exile attacks launched from American soil, which was borne from the U.S.–Cuba agreement following the Missile Crisis. What allowed many Cubans to achieve permanent resettlement was the adoption of the Cuban Adjustment Act in 1966, which changed the legal status of exiles from temporary refugees to permanent residents.

Exiles still had dreams of returning to a free Cuba one day, but they began to realize it would take some time. They turned

◀(From left to right) U.S. Senator Charles Schumer, Padrino (Parade Marshal) Max Gomez, and Governor George Pataki march in the 2002 Cuban Day Parade in New York City. Participating in parades and festivals are popular ways for Cuban Americans to celebrate their heritage, and are widely attended in New York, Miami, and other cities with Cuban American communities.

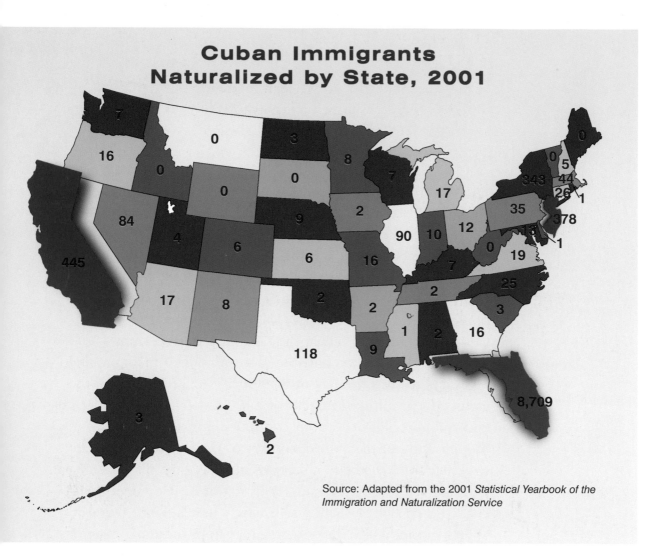

Cuban Immigrants Naturalized by State, 2001

7
0
3
0
16
0
0
8
7
17
343 0 5
44
26
1
84
4
6
9
2
90
10
12
35
378
13
445
17
8
6
16
7
0
19
1
2
2
25
3
1
2
16
118
9

Source: Adapted from the 2001 *Statistical Yearbook of the Immigration and Naturalization Service*

3

2

8,709

their attention to buying homes and seeking better-paying professional jobs, but it was not easy. Not every exile was a high-powered, well-educated professional. Those who had struggled to make a living in Cuba generally struggled at first in North America, too. And many did not speak English well enough to work in their professions in the United States.

In 1961 the federal government began to provide assistance with the Cuban Refugee Program. In its 20 years of existence the program had aided exiles with medical care, clothing, food, and social services though many say it was more than paid back through the economic contributions of successful Cuban exiles.

The Boom of the
Cuban American Community

The Cuban success story began in great part with small mom-and-pop shops. Homesick exiles wanted a taste of Cuba, whether it was a recording of Cuban-style *son* music or the down-home flavor of rice and beans. A handful of entrepreneurs set out to meet that demand. When they could not find American food distributors who carried *yucca* or *malanga* (tubers that are staples in the Cuban diet), they found out where that kind of produce was grown in Latin America and imported it. If mainstream supermarkets did not stock Cuban bread, they had Cuban bakers make it themselves.

Later, entrepreneurs extended their businesses beyond Cuban products and stores. They began to open florists, auto mechanic shops, furniture stores, and funeral parlors. By the middle of the decade, a neighborhood of southwest Miami became so Cubanized it became known as "Little Havana." It was filled with Cuban restaurants, bodegas, and other retail shops. In the

A Cuban hairstylist at work in his Little Havana salon in Miami. In the early 1960s, Cubans began opening up salons, shops, and restaurants all over the city's southwest section, which eventually became known as "Little Havana."

professional community, Cuban doctors, pharmacists, accountants, dentists, and lawyers began to pass the tests that gave them the credentials to work in the United States.

As years passed, Cuban-owned businesses expanded. Owners of small bodegas turned their stores into supermarkets, which then became supermarket chains. Investors began to build small factories and buy real estate. Some who had been top banking executives in Cuba opened banks in Miami. These bankers played a key role in the Cuban community's growth.

Most businessmen had little capital to start or expand a business because the Castro government had taken their property and money when they left Cuba. As a result, they had little or no collateral with which to qualify for a new loan. But at a crucial point the Cuban bankers stepped in, offering what were called "character loans" to Cuban investors based on the bankers' personal knowledge of the applicants and their business know-how. This system saw great results in Miami, as the loans that were used to build businesses helped form the base of what is now the city's multibillion-dollar economy.

During that same period, similar developments were occurring in the New Jersey towns of Union City and West New York. Located in northern Hudson County, across the Hudson River from New York City, the region has been a magnet for newcomers since the middle of the 19th century. German immigrants first arrived there, followed by Irish and Italian immigrants in the early 1900s. A majority who settled there worked in the embroidery factories that dotted the two towns.

A number of individuals from each immigrant group found economic success, and during the mid-1960s they left the gritty streets of Union City and West New York for the comforts and green lawns of the suburbs. During this mass relocation, many Cubans began to arrive to the area in large numbers.

The Italian American exodus left Bergenline Avenue, a main thoroughfare, virtually deserted. Stores were shuttered and windows were whitewashed, but Cuban immigrants soon arrived and brought the area back to life. They revived the district by opening stores that catered to the things exiles needed, from Cuban sandwich shops to grocery stores to restaurants. By the late 1970s and early 1980s, the majority of stores on Bergenline Avenue were owned by Cubans.

With the large-scale development of the 1960s—the new Cuban shops, Cuban restaurants, Cuban professional services, and Spanish-language television and radio shows—immigrants could now immerse themselves almost entirely in Cuban culture.

The Milkman Who Led the Way

It is not surprising that so many Cuban exiles ended up in Miami. After all, the city is located only 200 miles (322 km) from Cuba, and both places have similarly warm weather as well as tropical features like the majestic royal palm trees.

But how did 100,000 Cubans wind up in far-off North Hudson, in the towns of Union City and West New York? If some immigrants were willing to head north, why not New York City, which is better known as a historic exile destination? The answer to that question can be traced back to one immigrant couple from Fomento, a small town in the Las Villas province of central Cuba.

In 1949, newlyweds Manuel and Lydia Rodríguez spent their honeymoon in Miami Beach, where they befriended an Italian American woman. She lived in North Hudson but was spending the summer as a waitress in a local hotel. When the Rodríguezes' vacation ended, they did not go back to Cuba but instead drove north with their new American friend to North Hudson, where they decided to resettle.

Soon the Rodríguez couple opened their own milk delivery business. Friends from Fomento, impressed by the Rodríguezes' success, made their way to Union City, too. By the mid-1950s there was an estimated 2,000 to 3,000 Cubans in the area. It had become such a well-known destination that Fidel Castro visited it in 1955 during a fund-raising tour of Cuban communities in the United States.

The Cuban businesses and organizations established in the 1950s helped attract tens of thousands of exiles after Castro took power. Today there is still a Fomento Social Club right off the main shopping district, a reminder of the first Cubans who settled in the area more than half a century ago.

Cubans had great success in re-creating their homeland, not only in Miami, where the palm trees, the weather, and even the Spanish-style architecture were reminiscent of Cuba, but also in far-off New Jersey, with its cold winters and gray brick buildings that called up few memories of the Cuban landscape.

The One-and-a-Halfers

The generation that had brought families to the United States in the 1960s generally remained Cuban. The transplanted communities they had created allowed them to preserve many facets of their lives in Cuba: they read Cuban newspapers, listened to Cuban radio stations, and ate at Cuban restaurants.

The Dialogue

One of the most controversial crises of Cuban exile history was El Diálogo (the Dialogue), which occurred in the late 1970s. The "dialogue" in this case was between Cuban exiles and the Castro government. After the 1959 revolution, exile leaders maintained a policy of opposing any negotiation with the regime. They believed that while talks would give the impression of improved relations, they would ultimately not promote democracy. But in 1977, a faction of exiles decided to disregard that policy. It initiated secret negotiations with the Cuban government, which agreed to release some political prisoners and, for the first time since Castro became president, allow exiles to visit the island. When the negotiations were made public, many exiles grew distressed by the news.

There were protest marches in Washington, D.C., and in the Cuban centers of Miami and North Hudson. Businesses that were owned by exiles involved in El Diálogo were boycotted. Travel agencies that organized trips to Cuba were bombed, and at least two prominent *dialogueros* were killed. A terrorist group that called itself Omega 7 took responsibility for the murders.

By the mid-1980s the FBI had caught and imprisoned most of the violent anti-Diálogo militants. The killings and bombings stopped, and so did El Diálogo. To some, the negotiations succeeded in that dozens of long-held political prisoners were released, and a number of exiles were able to visit relatives back in Cuba. However, others argue that El Diálogo did nothing to change the regime's unjust policies.

But in the early 1970s, the situation began to change for the Cuban community in the United States. The children of the original exiles, who by this period were teenagers or college students, were becoming the first truly Cuban *American* generation. This group has been called "the one-and-a-halfers." (The parents, the original exiles, are "first generation" because they were the first to come to America. The children are not considered "second generation" because even if they spent most of their lives in the United States, they were born in Cuba.)

By definition, the one-and-a-halfers were situated somewhere between generations, the products of two cultures. Because they had grown up in Cuban neighborhoods, they learned Spanish and grew familiar with the food, music, and traditions of Cuban culture. But their neighborhoods were not complete beyond the influence of American culture. The one-and-a-halfers often spoke English better than Spanish, dressed in American-style clothes, and in some cases were as likely to eat hamburger and fries from a fast-food chain as a traditional Cuban meal of *arroz con pollo* (chicken with rice).

The one-and-a-halfers who attended college began to graduate in the late 1970s and early 1980s, at a time when it was becoming clear that the elder generation had achieved remarkable success over a short time. Owing in great part to the hard work and dedication of that generation, by 1979 more than 60 percent of Cuban families owned their homes. In Miami, more than one-third of all businesses were Cuban-owned.

This next generation brought up in the United States followed in the footsteps of its elders. After facing the chaos of the Mariel crisis, and the challenges of helping to settle 125,000 fellow Cubans, the one-and-a-halfers continued to develop a Cuban American identity. Their unique perspective was shaped by their American schooling and experiences in the U.S. workplace. They became more knowledgeable about American culture, and more comfortable in the wider English-speaking world outside their ethnic community.

One result of their efforts was their elections to political office. During the 1980s, in the cities of Miami, the nearby city of Hialeah, and Union City, New Jersey, Cuban Americans were elected mayors. By the early 1990s, there were three Cuban Americans in Congress—Ileana Ros-Lehtinen and Lincoln Díaz-Balart, Republicans from South Florida, and Democrat Robert Menéndez, from Union City. Díaz-Balart's brother, Mario, joined the group of representatives when he was elected in 2002. Other public figures of the one-and-a-half generation have led Cuban advocacy groups. One such individual is Jorge Mas, head of the Cuban American National Foundation (CANF) between 1981 and 1997. Considered the most influential anti-Castro group, CANF helped lobby for the U.S. trade embargo of Cuba, first implemented in 1960.

The one-and-a-halfers have made contributions in many other ways. In Miami, they are among the city's leading political figures, business executives, academics, journalists, and artists.

A group of young Cuban Americans enjoy the Miami beach. Children of the first waves of Cuban exiles are generally more Americanized than their parents and more comfortable in English-speaking environments beyond Little Havana and other Cuban neighborhoods.

Today the U.S. Cuban-born population is close to the national average in terms of home ownership, income, health, and education. The unemployment and poverty rate of Cuban Americans is lower than that of Puerto Ricans, Mexican Americans, and other Hispanic groups.

One ironic outcome of Cuban American success has been a waning Cuban influence on the communities of Union City and West New York. As the younger generation of Cuban Americans in those towns have graduated from college and attained high-salary jobs, like previous generations they have moved to suburban towns with smaller ethnic communities. Meanwhile, the parents of younger Cuban Americans have moved to Miami, further decreasing the Cuban population of North Hudson. The 2000 census recorded only 33,901 residents of Cuban origin in Hudson County, down from the almost 100,000 of the community's heyday during the early 1980s. The situation is the reverse in Miami: the city receives an increasing number of Cuban American college graduates from Hudson County, many who are younger than their predecessors.

A Growing Cuban Canadian Community

Cubans living in Canada face circumstances much different than Cubans living in the United States. Because there are smaller numbers of Cubans in Canada (and a majority of them still newcomers), a centralized immigrant community has not yet developed. There are no predominantly Cuban neighborhoods in Canada, not even in multicultural Toronto, the city with the largest number of Cuban residents. Subsequently, there are few Cuban restaurants and record shops to remind newcomers of the tastes and sounds of home.

However, the Cuban immigrants' current situation in Canada does not mean that they are in danger of losing their culture. More Cubans arrive in Canada every year, making it easy for the younger generations to grow up bicultural, as older Cuban American generations have done in the United States.

5 OLD TRADITIONS LOST AND KEPT

Like other people who left their country to settle in a new land, Cubans brought their nation's traditions to the United States. Some of those customs were lost, while others were kept and were even adopted by non-Cubans. Conversely, Cubans have also embraced several American traditions.

Traditions Lost

Old Cuba inherited from Spain the tradition of the siesta, a long lunch break in the middle of the day. People would leave their work places in the afternoon and eat a long, leisurely *almuerzo*, a full-blown mid-day dinner. After the *almuerzo*, Cubans would go home and take a nap before returning to work two or three hours later.

The rapid pace of life in the United States makes a siesta next to impossible. Whether Americans work in factories, offices, stores, or outdoors, they typically get one hour for lunch, sometimes less. So Cuban newcomers have had to adjust. Still, though the siesta is no more, some people, particularly elders, continue to have a large *almuerzo* in the afternoon instead of a light lunch. It often is the main meal of the day.

Another tradition that did not survive the migration to America completely intact is the Carnaval celebration, a festival popular in most Hispanic nations. The merrymaking of

◀ Schoolchildren line up for a Three Kings Day Parade in New York City. The holiday, popular in Cuban communities, commemorates the three kings of the Gospels who brought frankincense, gold, and myrrh to the baby Jesus.

Carnaval takes place before the beginning of Lent, a religious season when Catholics are supposed to fast (New Orleans' Mardi Gras is an American version of Carnaval). Cuba's Carnaval has parades with floats, masquerades, and dancing to conga and other forms of traditional music.

Although it's not really a Carnaval, the Festival de la Calle Ocho (Eighth Street Festival) is a popular festival among Cubans. Celebrated in March, the festival is named for the

Flag-waving teenagers watch the Cuban Day Parade in New York. Other patriotic Cuban celebrations include the birthday of revolutionary José Martí; Grito de Yara (Cry of Yara), which remembers the Ten Years War with Spain; and Grito de Baire (Cry of Baire), which remembers the beginning of the War of Independence in 1895.

main thoroughfare of Miami's Little Havana. First held in 1978, it includes some Carnaval-like festivities such as floats, beauty pageants, and music; however, most of the action takes place on a stage rather than as a street parade, and the celebration also doesn't always coincide with Lent. Some of the most popular performers in the Spanish-speaking world have given concerts for this Miami festival, playing music from salsa to rock and pop *en español* (in Spanish). It may not be a Carnaval, exactly, but Festival de la Calle Ocho has become one of the largest celebrations of Hispanic culture in the United States, regularly attracting up to one million people.

One Cuban celebration that may be disappearing is El Día de los Tres Reyes Magos (Three Kings Day). In Spanish-speaking countries, the tradition was for children to receive gifts not on Christmas Day, and not from Santa Claus, but on Three Kings Day (January 6) from Melchor, Gaspar, and Baltasar—the Three Kings who, according to the Gospels, arrived to Bethlehem bringing gifts of frankincense, gold, and myrrh for the baby Jesus.

In North America, Cuban children typically get their gifts from Santa on Christmas. However, some families maintain the Three Kings tradition, and some communities even organize Tres Reyes Magos parades, with the Three Kings arriving on camels with sacks of toys.

Traditions Kept

The patriotic observances of Cuban history are, of course, not treated as official holidays in the United States and Canada, yet they continue to be observed in Cuban communities. These include January 28, the birthday of national hero José Martí in 1853; and February 24, Grito de Baire (Cry of Baire), marking the start of the War of Independence in 1895. Other important dates are May 20, commemorating Cuban Independence in 1902; October 10, Grito de Yara (Cry of Yara), which set off the Ten Years War against colonial Spain (1868–78); and December 7, the Cuban equivalent of

Memorial Day in the United States. This holiday marks the anniversary of the death of Antonio Maceo, one of the leading Cuban generals in the War of Independence who died in battle. The celebrations are usually marked with patriotic speeches and the singing of the Cuban and American national anthems.

There is also the anniversary of the Bay of Pigs invasion in mid-April. In Cuba, it is a triumphal celebration that marks the victory of Castro's army over the exiles of Brigade 2506. In America's Cuban communities, the perspective on the holiday is the exact opposite: veterans of Brigade 2506 hold somber observances to memorialize those who made the ultimate sacrifice in the invasion.

One religious holiday that Catholic Cuban Americans continue to maintain is September 8, La Virgen de la Caridad (Our Lady of Charity), commemorating Cuba's patron saint. It marks the day in the 1500s when, according to tradition, three fishermen in a small boat witnessed a miracle. They were about to be capsized in a tempest when they spotted a statue of the Virgin Mary floating in the storm-tossed waves, whereupon the storm immediately passed, and their lives were saved.

What many believe to be the original Virgin Mary statue can be found in a church in the Cuban town of El Cobre, near the city of Santiago. It is the destination of a pilgrimage held on September 8. Cuban communities in the United States observe the feast with a Catholic mass followed by a procession led by a statue of the Virgin. The largest and best known of these is held at the Hermita de la Caridad del Cobre, a Miami chapel that rests along Biscayne Bay. It has become the spiritual center of Cuban Catholics living in the United States.

The holiday of Christmas is, of course, observed in Cuban American communities, but not exactly in the fashion other Americans celebrate it. The most obvious difference is that the traditional meal is held on December 24, Christmas Eve, and not on Christmas Day itself. The food is distinctively Cuban, too. Families eat black beans with rice; boiled *yucca* in a Cuban sauce of garlic, olive oil, and lime juice; and roast pork marinated in

The Music of Cuba

One way Cubans in America keep their culture alive is through music. No cultural tradition of Cuba is more distinctive or more famous throughout the world than its music.

Like so many Cuban cultural forms, Cuban music started with a mixture of African and Spanish elements. Slaves would use boxes for drums and play the traditional rhythms of their African ancestors; musicians would play Spanish melodies on guitars and other stringed instruments over those rhythms, giving birth to what became Cuban music.

Cuban music has many styles, including *son*, *danzón*, *guajira*, mambo, and cha-cha. All of these styles are traditional, some decades old, yet they are alive and thriving in Cuban communities—in concerts, dance clubs, record shops, and on the radio. Cuban Americans listen to tunes sung by famous artists of the old days in Cuba, such as legendary singer Celia Cruz, or the more recent hits of Cuban American performers like Gloria Estefan. Combining Cuban rhythms with American pop or rock melodies, Estefan is the most popular among artists of Cuban heritage brought up in the United States.

There is also a recognizable Cuban influence in the world of jazz. Saxophonist Paquito D'Rivera and trumpet player Arturo Sandoval are two exiles whose combinations of Cuban rhythms with traditional jazz instrumentation have become known as "Latin jazz."

Cuban musicians perform at a Havana restaurant. Most genres of Cuban music intricately blend Spanish melodies and African rhythms.

Cuba's National Pastime

Baseball is the national pastime not only of the United States, but also of Cuba. Because of the game's popularity in both countries, the love for the game has been one tradition Cubans have found easy to preserve as immigrants.

Baseball was introduced to Cuba in 1864, when three Cuban students from Alabama's Springhill College returned to Havana with baseballs and bats. Soon after, brothers Nemesio and Ernesto Guilló and their friend Enrique Porto founded the Habana baseball club. Ten years later a rival club, Almendares, was formed. Baseball soon became hugely popular, and a professional Cuban league began play in 1878.

Seven years before the Cuban league formed, the first Cuban player, Esteban Bellán, made his appearance in the American leagues. Bellán was a shortstop for the Troy Haymakers, an old National Association team based in New York state. In 1911 Armando Marsans and Rafael Almeida joined the Cincinnati Reds as the first Cubans of the modern era to play major league baseball.

By the 1960s more than 100 Cubans had played in the American major leagues. Some of them were among the best players of their time, like pitchers Luis Tiant and Mike Cuellar, Minnesota Twins outfielder Tony Oliva (the only player to win batting titles in his first two major league seasons), and Cincinnati infielder Tony Pérez, the first Cuban player inducted to the Hall of Fame.

In the late 1960s the Castro regime severely curtailed the flow of players from Cuba to the majors. However, the number of Cubans increased again in the 1990s. At first, this new wave was made up of Cubans raised in the United States, such as José Canseco and Rafael Palmeiro. Later in the decade, players who had become stars in Cuba defected and joined major league teams, including Yankee pitcher Orlando Hernández and his brother Livan, also a pitcher.

garlic and spices such as cumin, oregano, and juice from special sour oranges. In places where the December weather is warm, such as Miami, the pig is roasted over a spit on an open fire. In colder American cities, Cubans follow the same recipe but roast the pig—or more likely a leg of pork—in the kitchen oven. For dessert, people eat *turrón*, a nut and honey bar that was first eaten in Spain and has been enjoyed for centuries.

Some Cuban traditions have been embraced by non-Cubans, especially in Miami, where eating a Cuban sandwich (ham, roast pork, and cheese on grilled Cuban bread) is about as common as eating a slice of pizza. Similarly, Miamians of all ethnic groups were used to drinking little cups of strong Cuban espresso long before espresso bars became commonplace in the rest of the country.

New Traditions

Cubans in the United States don't only enjoy the traditions and festivities they brought from their old country; they have also adopted American holidays, often giving them a Cuban twist. For instance, Cuban American families celebrate Thanksgiving even though the holiday is unknown in Cuba. Just like in other American homes, Cuban families gather around the table to give thanks and eat turkey. But the turkey is prepared Cuban style (in much the same way as the Christmas roast pork) and is often stuffed with rice and black beans.

Fourth of July picnics are also popular. The younger kids may eat hot dogs and hamburgers, just like in a typical American celebration, but there may also be Cuban dishes such as *congrí* (rice and red beans cooked together with spices) and *chorizo*, a sausage Cubans adopted from the Spanish.

6 A COMMUNITY'S CHALLENGES

According to the 2000 U.S. Census, 73 percent of Cuban Americans are high school graduates, which is not much smaller than the 88 percent of the general population that finished high school. Similarly, 23 percent of Cubans have a college degree, compared to 28 percent of all Americans. The median income in Cuban American households is $32,417, closer to the national median of $35,225 than for the median of Hispanics overall.

Still, the Cuban American community has problems to overcome, including persistent Cuban stereotypes as well as debates over immigration policy and bilingual government and education.

Language

In many American cities, speaking Spanish on a regular basis sometimes causes friction between Hispanics and their non-Hispanic neighbors, and Miami is no exception. There, because the Cuban community is so influential, Spanish is not restricted to a particular neighborhood or group of people. It can be heard everywhere, from the most run-down neighborhoods to the most exclusive clubs and restaurants. Among the older generation of business leaders, it remains the language of choice.

By the 1970s, there were so many Spanish-speaking Cubans in South Florida that Dade County, which includes Miami,

◀ Many Cuban families who have settled in U.S. cities and suburbs still face serious issues, including the continuing debates over bilingual education, immigration policy, and negative portrayals of Cubans in the media.

passed a law in 1973 making its government officially bilingual. Legal documents, voting ballots, and notices to citizens were all made available in both English and Spanish. Many Miamians who did not know Spanish opposed this law and overturned it in a referendum in November 1980. At that time the community was reeling from the sudden influx of 125,000 Cubans who arrived during the Mariel crisis. County government returned to conducting business in English only.

However, little changed in the everyday communication of Dade County residents. People continued to speak the language of their choice, which was Spanish for hundreds of thousands of older Cubans. In 1993, a new generation of Cuban Americans comfortable with both languages successfully pushed to make Dade officially bilingual again.

Tensions still remain between non-Hispanics and Hispanics. Some non-Hispanics believe speaking Spanish in front of people who do not know the language is inappropriate. They also fear Spanish will at some point "take over" English as the primary language of the United States. The counterargument of Cubans, as well as other Hispanics in Miami, is that speaking Spanish should not be considered anti-American. The Spanish language is, after all, an outgrowth of their immigrant heritage, which they are entitled to keep as Americans.

Another major language issue is the debate over the best approach to teaching English to Cuban children, a particularly hot topic in South Florida school districts. Some educators favor bilingual education, a method under which children attend English classes designed for those learning a new language, and take other subjects such as history or math in their native tongue. Then, when the students know English well enough, they switch over to regular classes taught in English. The intention of bilingual education has been to help students learn at a satisfactory pace in their subjects until they learn English.

Other educators are opposed to bilingual education, asserting that it does a poor job of teaching English and does not take advantage of young people's ability to easily pick up a new language. They also argue that many students never really learn English well enough to assimilate completely. As an alternative to bilingual education, they propose the English immersion system, under which students undergo intensive English-language courses for one or two years, and take their other subjects in English with students who already know English.

Yet a third system that educators have championed is called "dual immersion." In schools using this program, all students—whether they primarily speak English, Spanish, or another language—attend classes in English for one-half of the day, and then classes in another language for the day's other half. The goal is for everybody to learn two languages. Surprisingly, many on both sides of the bilingual education debate support dual immersion, though few schools offer the program.

In Miami, where most newly arrived Cuban children live, many schools offer bilingual programs. However, other communities favor immersion. The controversy is likely to continue in the years ahead.

Immigration

For years now, Cubans who arrive to the United States have benefited from special considerations not given to most immigrants. From the very beginning of the Castro revolution, Cuban immigrants have been permitted to stay in the United States. At first, the government allowed the original exiles in on a temporary basis, anticipating the fall of the Castro regime and the return of the exiles to their native country. But when President Lyndon Johnson signed the Cuban Adjustment Act in 1966, an unlimited number of Cubans were permitted to become permanent residents after living one year in the United States. (After five years, like other permanent residents they could apply to become American citizens.) As a result of the legislation, nearly all the refugees who arrived during the 1980 Mariel crisis were permitted to stay, even though they had no immigration papers. Only those discovered to have criminal records were not admitted and placed in detention.

Meanwhile, refugees from other countries have faced much stricter limits. Only a certain number of them may legally enter the United States each year. Those who do not enter through legal means and are caught by the authorities can be deported, or sent back, to their country of origin. The rationale for treating Cubans differently is that most immigrants who are deported generally do not face persecution in their home countries for having emigrated like Cubans do.

Still, other immigrants argue that immigration policy is following a double standard. Haitians, who form another large community in Miami, have been particularly angry. Many have arrived just like the Cubans in boats to flee repression and harsh poverty conditions. But they have been sent back, while Cubans have been permitted to stay.

It became more difficult for Cubans to enter the United States after the "rafter" crisis of 1994 and the "wet foot/dry foot" policy that the U.S. government implemented in the months afterward. The policy signaled a big change for Cuban exiles. Before it was drawn up, Cuban rafters were almost always allowed to stay even if they were intercepted at sea. The new policy still did not satisfy Haitians, who argued that Cubans who made it ashore were still being given preferential treatment over Haitians. And it did not please Cubans, who argued that the United States should not send people back to a place where they cannot live in freedom, whether they are caught at sea or on land.

Stereotypes

Cuban Americans often complain that they are portrayed negatively on television and in newspapers. Some say that they are depicted as relentless lobbyists who take advantage of their political clout to put pressure on Fidel Castro. The stereotype was raised more frequently during the crisis of six-year-old Elián González, which began in late 1999 and ended in June 2000.

Elián and his mother, Elisabet, attempted to flee to the United States on a small boat. She drowned during the journey, but Elián was rescued and turned over to an uncle who lived in Miami. Then Elián's father, Juan Miguel, who was divorced from Elián's mother but kept in touch with the boy, asked for his son to be sent back to Cuba. The Miami relatives, fearing that Juan Miguel was asking for the return of his son under pressure from the Castro regime, insisted that Juan Miguel had to personally come to get Elián in order for them to release him.

The drama of the little boy soon became the subject of a national obsession, covered by 24-hour cable-television news programs and international newspapers. The standoff between Elián's father and his relatives went on for months. Then, to the surprise of most exiles, Juan Miguel came to the United States

The story of six-year-old Elián González captured the interest of millions of Cubans and Americans. After a seven-month standoff, the Cuban boy was refused refugee status and returned to Cuba at his father's request.

to demand the return of Elián. In the meantime, thousands of Cuban Americans had gathered around the Little Havana home of Elián's relatives to support them.

To nearly every Cuban American, it was a heartrending conflict. Escaping Cuba and finding freedom in the United States was a sensitive issue to all Cuban exiles. What made the story even more compelling for those supporting Elián's relatives was the idea that the boy's mother had given her life so that he could live in America. It seemed inconceivable to many Cuban Americans that the very country that had provided that freedom would send the boy back to a father who—some believed—was indoctrinated or pressured by the Castro government. A number of Americans and, eventually, the Clinton Administration, viewed it differently: the boy's father wanted him back, and Elián belonged with him. In offices, in factories, and in just about every place of work in Miami, Cuban

An anti-Castro group demonstrates outside the home of Elián González' relatives in Miami, January 2000. Thousands of Cuban Americans in Miami and other communities supported Elián's relatives in their fight to let the boy remain in the United States.

Americans and others argued about what to do with Elián.

The standoff ended in April 2000, when armed federal agents stormed the house where Elián was staying and gave the boy back to his father. Shortly after, the Elián ordeal was over, but not the trauma it caused among Cuban Americans. Community and civic leaders feared the image that the rest of the country had of Cubans had been seriously harmed. They started publicity campaigns to present a better image of Cuban immigrants and the anti-Castro cause.

7 THE FUTURE OF CUBAN IMMIGRATION

The future of Cuban immigrants is greatly dependent on what will happen in Cuba after the end of the Castro regime. Will the same repressive system continue under different leaders? Or will there be a rebirth of democracy? Regardless of the final outcome, Cuban Americans will certainly be involved in shaping the island's future, even if the majority of them continue living in the United States.

Had the Castro government fallen in the 1960s or even in the 1970s, a large segment of the Cuban exiles would have probably gone back to Cuba. During those years just about every immigrant family had a desire to return. But attitudes have changed with the passing of decades. Today, despite their longing for their homeland, most Cubans would probably remain in the United States even if democracy came to Cuba. A large segment of the original exiles that would have returned when it was younger is now too settled in the United States to return. Most members of the younger generation of exiles, which have grown up to lead comfortable American lives, also would unlikely return.

Despite the intentions of many Cuban Americans to remain in the United States, their ties with Cuba will undoubtedly remain strong. They may even have the opportunity to use the expertise they have gained in the United States to help rebuild Cuba in the post-Castro era. While living in the United States they have learned how democracy works from the inside; some

◀ President George W. Bush meets with Cuban dissidents at the White House in May 2003. Bush is a popular leader among Cuban Americans, the majority of whom have voted for Republican presidential candidates since the early 1960s.

have learned first-hand how to start and expand a successful business. If the opportunity presented itself, they could perhaps help organize fair, open national elections after Castro is gone. Cuban business leaders could help put together a marketing plan to promote tourism to Cuba; political leaders could continue to develop U.S. policy regarding the country. However, one foreseeable problem of the Cuban Americans' efforts is the resentment some native Cubans may feel toward the exiles. They could object to the idea of "Americanized" Cubans telling them what to do.

Yet even many of those "Cuban" Cubans may still consider moving to the United States, although their reasons for leaving Cuba could differ from those of the present. Most Cuban Americans picture a democratic post-Castro state, in which case Cubans would no longer have to leave because they face persecution from the government.

Politics

In the years ahead, Cuban Americans are likely to remain an important political force and a crucial voting group in presidential elections. The majority of Cubans living in the United States are Republican. This trend dates back to the defeat of the exiles at the Bay of Pigs, which many Cubans blamed on the decision of President Kennedy, a Democrat, to not send American jet fighters during the invasion. Since then, many Cuban Americans have perceived Democratic policy as "soft" on Fidel Castro's regime.

According to voting polls, more than 80 percent of Cuban Americans voted for Republican presidential candidates Ronald Reagan and George H. W. Bush. Support for Republicans slipped in the 1996 election, during a time when some felt that the party supported anti-Hispanic, anti-immigrant policies. But in 2000 George W. Bush proved Republican leaders had renewed ties with Cuban Americans when he received about 80 percent of their vote in the presidential election against Vice President Al Gore. One reason attributed to Bush's success was

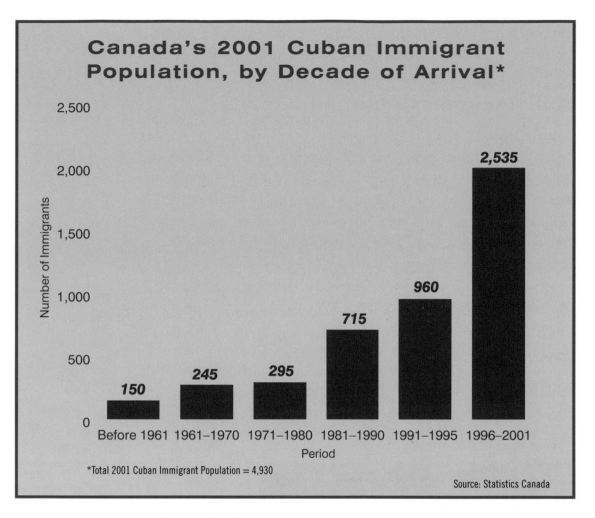

Canada's 2001 Cuban Immigrant Population, by Decade of Arrival*

Number of Immigrants

2,500

2,000 — 2,535

1,500

1,000 — 960

715

500 — 150 245 295

0

Before 1961 | 1961–1970 | 1971–1980 | 1981–1990 | 1991–1995 | 1996–2001

Period

*Total 2001 Cuban Immigrant Population = 4,930

Source: Statistics Canada

that he worked hard to overcome the existing anti-immigrant image of the Republican Party. Another equally important factor was the resentment Cuban Americans felt over the Clinton administration's decision to forcibly remove Elián González from his uncle's home and return him to his father. Many believed that they could express that resentment by voting against Clinton's partner.

Campaign strategists believe that the extra Cuban American votes that went to Bush helped tip him over the edge in the Florida state total, which in turn gave him the razor-thin margin in electoral votes he needed to become president. Today, politicians of both parties, realizing the key role that Cuban voters can play, are eager to court Cuban voters. They campaign in

HPHS Library

Cuban neighborhoods—sometimes giving speeches in Spanish—and promise to deal with the issues most important to Cuban voters.

The Youngest Cuban Americans

More than 40 years have passed since the first Cuban exodus began. The original generation of exiles has grown older; some individuals have watched their friends die without seeing Cuba again. Many of the exiles' sons and daughters—the first truly bicultural and bilingual generation—have become well established in their jobs, and have had children of their own. These children—babies, grammar school kids, teenagers—are the newest generation of Cuban Americans. Their grandparents remained wholly Cuban; many of their parents have only dim memories of Cuba, as they were very young when they left. This third generation, who only knows life in the United States, will play a decisive role in shaping the future of Cuban immigration.

Many Cuban American children who live outside Miami and other cities heavily populated by Cubans are enjoying a high level of assimilation in schools with few other Cuban or

A Cuban girl at work in a Catholic classroom in Little Havana, Florida. The youngest generation of Cuban Americans—to date the generation most assimilated in American society—will play a decisive role in the future of Cuban immigration to the United States.

Hispanic kids. At home these children may have Cuban meals, but beyond what they eat they may have few traits distinguishing them from other minority groups. They and their children several decades from now could perhaps be challenged to keep Cuban culture alive.

Even in Miami, a town soaked in Cuban atmosphere where Spanish can be heard everywhere, English is more often than not the youngest generation's language of choice. Cuban grandparents, who may not speak much English, sometimes have trouble communicating with their grandchildren.

Yet as the Cuban American community faces Americanization through its younger generation, another group, the newcomers, promises to preserve Cuban culture. This group includes the more than 30,000 who came during the "rafter" crisis and the thousands who have arrived since. The group's members may be adults in their 30s or 40s, teenagers, or young children; all prefer speaking Spanish and are more thoroughly Cuban. Their presence in the Cuban communities of the United States assures that the immigrant population remains diverse in the years ahead.

In Canada, the relatively new Cuban community of Canada is just beginning a similar transformation. It will never be large enough to shape Canadian culture, politics, and economics in the manner that the 1.2 million Cuban Americans have done in the United States. Nonetheless, if the success of bicultural Cuban Americans is an indicator of what is possible in another country, there will eventually be a generation of successful, bicultural Cuban Canadians.

Until the day when the Cuban government implements radical changes, or the communist system collapses altogether, Cubans will continue a tradition now nearly 200 years old— dating back to the colonial struggle against Spain—of seeking the freedom in the United States and Canada they cannot find at home.

FAMOUS CUBAN AMERICANS/CANADIANS

Desi Arnaz (1917–86), costar with wife Lucille Ball of the hugely popular 1950s TV sitcom *I Love Lucy*. Arnaz was also a producer and director, and was the first to use a three-camera studio setup, a practice that became standard in television production.

Celia Cruz (1925–2003), veteran salsa singer who first became a star in Cuba in the 1950s and later sought exile in the United States, where she continued her career.

Gloria Estefan (1958–), Grammy-winning singer who, along with her husband and record producer Emilio Estefan, combined Cuban rhythms with American pop melodies to sell more than 70 million albums worldwide. She has recorded albums in Spanish as well as in English.

Andy García (1956–), critically acclaimed actor, known for his performances in *The Untouchables*, *Internal Affairs*, and *The Godfather: Part III*, for which he received an Oscar nomination.

Roberto Goizueta (1931–97), former chief executive officer of the Coca-Cola Company and one of the most admired executives in the business world. During his tenure as Coca-Cola's chief, which began in 1981, he raised the company's market value by 3,500 percent.

Oscar Hijuelos (1951–), author who won the Pulitzer Prize in 1989 for *The Mambo Kings Play Songs of Love*. The novel, which was adapted into a movie in 1992, tells the story of Cuban musicians in New York in the early 1950s, when Latin music became popular in the United States.

Jorge Mas Canosa (1939–97), chairman of the Cuban American National Foundation who became hugely influential in helping to shape U.S. policy regarding the Castro regime.

Atanasio ("Tony") Pérez (1941–), first Cuban major-league baseball player inducted into the National Baseball Hall of Fame. In his career that spanned from 1964 to 1986, he hit 379 home runs and had 1,652 runs batted in.

Ileana Ros-Lehtinen (1952–), Republican Congresswoman and Chair of the Subcommittee on International Operations and Human Rights. In 1989 she became the first Cuban American elected to the U.S. Congress.

GLOSSARY

abolitionist—a person in favor of ending slavery.

bodega—a grocery store that specializes in Hispanic foods.

Cold War—the period of rivalry between the U.S. and the Soviet Union, from 1945 to 1990, during which there was no open fighting but much political and economic conflict.

collateral—property used to secure a debt.

communist—follower of a political and economic philosophy under which goods and services are produced by a government that prohibits private enterprise and restricts political and individual rights.

dissidents—those who disagree with the established political system.

deportation—when immigration authorities formally remove someone from the United States or Canada.

elite—a small group of people who exercise their influence on a country.

embargo—a government prohibition on trade with another country.

exiles—people who leave their nation for political reasons.

expropriate—to take private property or money that is then used by the government.

exodus—a departure of a large number of people from a place.

golpe de estado—a violent change of government.

indoctrinate—to teach an ideology with the goal of discouraging independent thought.

pilgrimage—a journey to a sacred place.

protectorate—a country over which a foreign power has authority.

socioeconomic—having to do with social and economic factors.

subsidy—a grant of money from one country to another, or from a government to a private company or organization.

FURTHER READING

Antón, Alex, and Roger E. Hernández. *Cubans in America*. New York: Kensington Books, 2002.

Balido, Gisselle. *Cubantime: A Celebration of Cuban Life in America*. New York: Silver Lining Books, 2001.

Benson, Michael. *Gloria Estefan*. Minneapolis, Minn.: Lerner Publishing Group, 1998.

Conde, Yvonne M. *Operation Pedro Pan: The Untold Exodus of 14,048 Cuban Children*. New York: Routledge, 2000.

Fernández Barrios, Flor. *Blessed by Thunder: Memoir of a Cuban Girlhood*. Seattle, Wash.: Seal Press, 1999.

García, María Cristina. *Havana USA.* Berkeley: University of California Press, 1997.

González Pando, *Miguel. The Cuban Americans*. Westport, Conn.: Greenwood Publishing Group, 1998.

Pérez Firmat, *Gustavo. Life on the Hyphen: The Cuban-American Way.* Austin: University of Texas Press, 1994.

Suárez, Virgil. *Spared Angola: Memories from a Cuban-American Childhood.* Houston, Tex.: Arte Público Press, 1997.

Veciana-Suárez, Ana. *Flight to Freedom.* London: Orchard Books, 2002.

INTERNET RESOURCES

http://www.canfnet.org

The homepage of the Cuban American National Foundation, which supports the suspension of relations between Cuba and the United States until Fidel Castro's dictatorship ends.

http://www.cambiocubano.com

This page charts the recent events of the activist group Cambio Cubano, which believes that renewed trade between the United States and Cuba will help to peacefully change the Fidel Castro regime.

http://www.lanuevacuba.com/megalinks.htm

A site with a comprehensive list of links to Cuban American sites.

http://www.cnc.org

The homepage of the Cuban American National Council, which provides "education, housing and community development services to needy individuals" in the Greater Miami area.

http://www.miami.edu/iccas/iccas.htm

The University of Miami's Institute for Cuban and Cuban-American Studies serves as a resource center for those doing research on Cuban Americans and other related topics.

http://www.cuban-exile.com

The Cuban Information Archives is a fascinating collection of primary source materials pertaining to anti-Castro Cuban exile activities and developments.

http://www.cubagenweb.org/index.htm

A site entailing genealogical resources for those looking for their Cuban and Spanish roots.

Publisher's Note: The websites listed on this page were active at the time of publication. The publisher is not responsible for websites that have changed their address or discontinued operation since the date of publication. The publisher reviews and updates the websites each time the book is reprinted.

INDEX

Numbers in **bold italic** refer to captions.

INDEX

INDEX

CONTRIBUTORS

SENATOR EDWARD M. KENNEDY has represented Massachusetts in the United States Senate for more than 40 years. Kennedy serves on the Senate Judiciary Committee, where he is the senior Democrat on the Immigration Subcommittee. He currently is the ranking member on the Health, Education, Labor and Pensions Committee in the Senate, and also serves on the Armed Services Committee, where he is a member of the Senate Arms Control Observer Group. He is also a member of the Congressional Friends of Ireland and a trustee of the John F. Kennedy Center for the Performing Arts in Washington, D.C.

Throughout his career, Kennedy has fought for issues that benefit the citizens of Massachusetts and the nation, including the effort to bring quality health care to every American, education reform, raising the minimum wage, defending the rights of workers and their families, strengthening the civil rights laws, assisting individuals with disabilities, fighting for cleaner water and cleaner air, and protecting and strengthening Social Security and Medicare for senior citizens.

Kennedy is the youngest of nine children of Joseph P. and Rose Fitzgerald Kennedy, and is a graduate of Harvard University and the University of Virginia Law School. His home is in Hyannis Port, Massachusetts, where he lives with his wife, Victoria Reggie Kennedy, and children, Curran and Caroline. He also has three grown children, Kara, Edward Jr., and Patrick, and four grandchildren.

Senior consulting editor STUART ANDERSON served as Executive Associate Commissioner for Policy and Planning and Counselor to the Commissioner at the Immigration and Naturalization Service from August 2001 until January 2003. He spent four and a half years on Capitol Hill on the Senate Immigration Subcommittee, first for Senator Spencer Abraham and then as Staff Director of the subcommittee for Senator Sam Brownback. Prior to that, he was Director of Trade and Immigration Studies at the Cato Institute in Washington, D.C., where he produced reports on the history of immigrants in the military and the role of immigrants in high technology. He currently serves as Executive Director of the National Foundation for American Policy, a nonpartisan public policy research organization focused on trade, immigration, and international relations. He has an M.A. from Georgetown University and a B.A. in Political Science from Drew University. His articles have appeared in such publications as the *Wall Street Journal*, *New York Times*, and *Los Angeles Times*.

MARIAN L. SMITH served as the senior historian of the U.S. Immigration and Naturalization Service (INS) from 1988 to 2003, and is currently the immigration and naturalization historian within the Department of Homeland Security in Washington, D.C. She studies, publishes, and speaks on the history of the immigration agency and is active in the management of official 20th-century immigration records.

PETER HAMMERSCHMIDT is the First Secretary (Financial and Military Affairs) for the Permanent Mission of Canada to the United Nations. Before taking this position, he was a ministerial speechwriter and policy specialist for the Department of National

CONTRIBUTORS

Defence in Ottawa. Prior to joining the public service, he served as the Publications Director for the Canadian Institute of Strategic Studies in Toronto. He has a B.A. (Honours) in Political Studies from Queen's University, and an MScEcon in Strategic Studies from the University of Wales, Aberystwyth. He currently lives in New York, where in his spare time he operates a freelance editing and writing service, Wordschmidt Communications.

Manuscript reviewer ESTHER OLAVARRIA serves as General Counsel to Senator Edward M. Kennedy, ranking Democrat on the U.S. Senate Judiciary Committee, Subcommittee on Immigration. She is Senator Kennedy's primary advisor on immigration, nationality, and refugee legislation and policies. Prior to her current job, she practiced immigration law in Miami, Florida, working at several nonprofit organizations. She cofounded the Florida Immigrant Advocacy Center and served as managing attorney, supervising the direct service work of the organization and assisting in the advocacy work. She also worked at Legal Services of Greater Miami, as the directing attorney of the American Immigration Lawyers Association Pro Bono Project, and at the Haitian Refugee Center, as a staff attorney. She clerked for a Florida state appellate court after graduating from the University of Florida Law School. She was born in Havana, Cuba, and raised in Florida.

Reviewer JANICE V. KAGUYUTAN is Senator Edward M. Kennedy's advisor on immigration, nationality, and refugee legislation and policies. Prior to working on Capitol Hill, Ms. Kaguyutan was a staff attorney at the NOW Legal Defense and Education Fund's Immigrant Women Program. Ms. Kaguyutan has written and trained extensively on the rights of immigrant victims of domestic violence, sexual assault, and human trafficking. Her previous work includes representing battered immigrant women in civil protection order, child support, divorce, and custody hearings, as well as representing immigrants before the Immigration and Naturalization Service on a variety of immigration matters.

ROGER E. HERNÁNDEZ is the most widely read nationally syndicated columnist writing on Hispanic American issues and is coauthor of *Cubans in America*, an illustrated history of the Cuban presence in the United States. He also teaches journalism and English composition at Rutgers University and the New Jersey Institute of Technology, where he is Writer-in-Residence.

PICTURE CREDITS

3:     Zoran Milich/Getty Images
Chapter Icon: PhotoDisc, Inc.
14:    U.S. Department of Defense
17:    © OTTN Publishing
19:    Robert van der Hilst/Corbis
20:    Hulton/Archive/Getty Images
22:    Hulton/Archive/Getty Images
25:    Bettmann/Corbis
26:    Hulton/Archive/Getty Images
29:    (left) John Fitzgerald Kennedy
       Library
29:    (right) Hulton/Archive/Getty
       Images
32:    Tim Chapman/*Miami Herald*/Getty
       Images
33:    © OTTN Publishing
34:    Roger Lemoyne/Liaison/Getty
       Images
36:    U.S. Coast Guard/Getty Images
40:    Lyndon B. Johnson Presidential
       Library
43:    Alex Wong/Getty Images
46:    Hulton/Archive/Getty Images
49:    Hulton/Archive/Getty Images

50:    © OTTN Publishing
54:    Hulton/Archive/Getty Images
61:    Tim Chapman/*Miami Herald*/Getty
       Images
65:    Stephen Ferry/Liaison/Getty
       Images
66:    U.S. Department of Defense
68:    AFP/Getty Images
70:    Monika Graff/Getty Images
72:    © OTTN Publishing
73:    Tony Arruza/Corbis
78:    Robert Nickelsberg/Liaison/Getty
       Images
80:    Mario Tama/Getty Images
82:    Monika Graff/Getty Images
85:    Bob Krist/Corbis
88:    Robert Nickelsberg/Liaison/Getty
       Images
93:    Joe Raedle/Getty Images
94:    Robert Nickelsberg/Getty Images
96:    Stefan Zaklin/Getty Images
99:    © OTTN Publishing
100:   Nathan Benn/Corbis

Cover: Christopher Brown/PictureQuest; **back cover:** Monika Graff